Poverty in India

Edited by

K.R. Gupta

ATLANTIC

PUBLISHERS & DISTRIBUTORS (P) LTD

Published by

ATLANTIC

PUBLISHERS & DISTRIBUTORS (P) LTD

B-2, Vishal Enclave, Opp. Rajouri Garden,
New Delhi-110027
Phones : +91-11-25413460, 25429987, 25466842

Sales Office
7/22, Ansari Road, Darya Ganj,
New Delhi-110002
Phones : +91-11-23273880, 23275880, 23280451
Fax : +91-11-23285873
web : www.atlanticbooks.com
e-mail : info@atlanticbooks.com

Chennai Branch
5, Nallathambi Street, Wallajah Road,
Chennai-600002
Phones : +91-44-64611085, 32413319
e-mail : chennai@atlanticbooks.com

ISBN 978-81-269-0900-1

Printed in India
at Nice Printing Press, Delhi

Preface

The past century has been marked by the transformation of India from a colonial, agrarian economy into a modern industrialising, knowledge-based economy within the framework of a liberal and secular democracy. Indeed, India is on the threshold of great power status. Commentators both at home and abroad are extolling India's dramatic rise. Goldman Sachs' Economic Research Report on Global Economics, released in January 2007, even speaks of India becoming the second largest economy after China by 2050. India is now getting used to its much higher rate of growth, first around 6 per cent a year, and now 8 per cent, occasionally touching even 9 per cent. In the last quarter of financial year 2006-07 the economy grew at 9.7 per cent. As a consequence of this sustained span of economic expansion, the country now boasts of a middle class variously estimated between 150 and 300 million. Many of the country's infrastructural bottlenecks, which had clogged economic growth, have now been addressed or are at least being ameliorated. There is a long list of achievements, sufficient enough to be celebrated and to hope that the dream of great power status is now within realisation. However, before one joins in the chorus of celebration, it might be desirable to take stock of poverty—one of the chief infirmities that still stalk India's economy.

Though rapid economic growth has meant some decline in both rural and urban poverty, about 260 million people (26 per cent of the total population) still remain below the official poverty line—this class lives on less than two dollars a day. There is an ever-widening gap between poor people and those who are better off. There is an equally convincing set of data relating to the various dimensions of poverty to show that we have a long way to go—a whopping 350 million people are illiterate, 150 million lack access to drinking water, 750 million lack decent sanitation, 50 per cent of the children eat below acceptable nutritional levels, and basic medicines are unavailable in 75 per cent of the villages. The widespread undernourishment in general and child malnutrition in particular are at shocking level. While life expectancy at birth has no doubt risen to 63 years, infant mortality rate (IMR) and maternal mortality rate (MMR) are still at unacceptably high levels—57 per 1000 and 301 per 1,00,000 live births respectively; IMR is even worse than that of Bangladesh. In terms of Human Development Index, India is ranked 126th among 177 listed countries of the world. Merely citing this dire statistic, however, does not adequately capture the sheer destitution and misery of this segment of the populace. The poverty that they endure robs them of their human dignity and mocks even commonplace notions of social justice and equity. A great power like India can ill afford to consign virtually a quarter of its citizenry to a condition of such near endemic poverty.

Growth, when unevenly spread, dwarfs overall prosperity. Hence, bridging the income divide is the biggest challenge for India. Economic growth must be inclusive and touch all sections of the society. Egalitarian reforms need to be taken to ensure that the full benefit of economic liberalisation reaches people at all levels. Reduction of poverty has been one of the guiding principles of planning process in India. The role of economic growth for providing more employment avenues to the population has been clearly recognized. The growth-oriented approach has been reinforced by focusing on specific sectors which offer greater opportunities to the people to participate in the growth process. Special programmes have been taken up by the Central and State Governments for the weaker and underprivileged sections of society like Food for Work and National Rural Employment Programme have been launched to use the unemployed to generate productive assets and build rural infrastructure. The other important initiatives include National Rural Employment Guarantee Scheme, Bharat Nirman, Jawaharlal Nehru National Urban Renewal Mission, Sarva Shiksha Abhiyan, National Social Assistance Programme (provides old age pension to destitute persons of 65 years and above), Sampoorna Grameen Rozgar Yojana, Indira Awaas

Yojana and many more. Approach Paper to the Eleventh Five-Year Plan has clearly laid down that these programmes are important complements to the general strategy of accelerating growth and making it broad-based and hence, need to be strengthened and made more effective during the Eleventh Plan.

Eminent contributors to the present anthology analyse the persisting problem of poverty in India in true dimensions through their well-researched valuable articles. The factors responsible for poverty and the measures taken by the Indian government to eradicate it have been analysed. Poverty in urban and rural areas has been individually studied; case studies of various Indian cities in this direction have also been given. Urban poverty and its alleviation schemes adopted in several developing and developed countries have also been studied, which would certainly help the Indian policymakers to apply the same to our country, if feasible, and thereby reduce, if not eradicate poverty. The papers primarily focus on the fact that if India is to realise its true potential to eradicate poverty and thereby become a developed country with its own position in the comity of nations, it has to enhance its investment in the health and education sector; create new employment opportunities for all, particularly those in rural areas; eliminate the rural-urban divide and develop infrastructure both in rural as well as urban areas.

It is hoped that the present book will prove useful to all those persons who are concerned with the overall development of the nation. It is an invaluable reference source for students and teachers of Economics and researchers on this subject. In addition, the policymakers responsible for formulation and execution of economic policies, planners, government agencies and NGOs will find this book extremely informative and useful. It is highly recommended for parliamentarians at the centre and legislators at the state capitals for informed debates on policy options for poverty reduction in India.

I express my sincere gratitude to all the contributors to this Volume who worked hard to present their learned papers, which have enriched the anthology.

K.R. GUPTA

Contents

Measuring Global Poverty: India on 20 cents a Day*

1

Aseem Shrivastava

Global poverty estimates report the number of people living on less than $1 or $2 a day. But purchasing power (dis)parities suggest that it could be more accurate to say that the poor in countries like India are living on less than $0.20 or $0.40 a day.

The World Bank—which has to be applauded for having made the first such attempt—started making international comparisons of poverty only about two decades ago. For obvious reasons of convenience it developed two simple notions of poverty. The US Treasury being the power behind the institution, and the dollar being the reserve currency by design, the lower poverty line was set at $1 a day per capita. Those below it were considered "the poorest of the poor". The upper poverty line was set at $2 a day. Those living on $1-2 a day were still poor, but not as badly off. The updated numbers today, corrected for inflation, are $1.08 and $2.15.

The Vagaries of Purchasing Power (Dis)Parities

However, there was a problem. It was realised that $1 goes much farther in purchasing necessary items of consumption in a poor country compared to a rich one. (Moreover, exchange rates do not take into account non-traded goods.) Using prevailing exchange rates, Rs. 45 can buy more in India than $1 can in America. So unless it was corrected for the lower cost of living in poor countries—enabling access to a bigger amount of real goods for the same amount of money—this measure of

---

* *Courtesy*: southasia.oneworld.net. and www.infochangeindia.org

poverty was likely to give an overestimate of the number of poor people living in absolute poverty. To make purchasing power across countries comparable, economists developed what is known as the PPP (purchasing power parity) index. Taking into account the lower cost of living in impoverished countries, a conversion factor is now applied to market exchange rates to calculate what is minimally necessary to survive there.

Using widely quoted World Bank numbers on GDP, this conversion factor for a country like India (2005) can be computed to be approximately 5.3. This means that $1.08 a day in India should effectively imply a purchasing power of about 20 cents a day to an American – or indeed anyone – unacquainted with the nuances of PPP calculations. However, given how the numbers are quoted everywhere, the dominant impression that is conveyed is that the poor are living on less than $1 or $2 a day when, in fact, it would be enormously more accurate, as far as everyday English is concerned, to say that the poor are living on less than $0.20 or $0.40 a day. The reason why this is not done is obvious: it would give an even more alarming picture of the scale and depth of poverty across this enormously wealthy world. Most decent people are shocked enough by the understated numbers in the form they are widely quoted. More reality would numb and paralyse even the grittiest of activists. "Humanity," T. S. Eliot wrote, "cannot bear much reality." He had the privileged in mind.

The most recent World Bank estimates for India are based on household surveys carried out in 1999-2000. It was found that almost 80% of purported superpower India's population was surviving on less than $2.15 a day (in PPP terms). That is, about 800 million people were living on $0.40 a day or less. Nearly 35% (350 million) were found to be living on $0.20 a day or less. Even if the proportion of poor people has fallen somewhat during the past five to six years, the absolute numbers would not look too different today.

During the course of survey several non-experts abroad who have traveled to India, and are thus somewhat familiar with market exchange rates, have been asked how they interpret the $1 a day or $2 a day figure. The answer is: literally. In other words, they think that really poor Indians (35% of the population) live on less than Rs. 45 and less poor Indians (another 45% of the population) live on between Rs. 45-90 a day. In their imagination that is bad enough for Western countries to send aid to poor countries.

However, if their belief was in fact correct then (assuming Rs. 20 a day to be the minimum needed to supply the 2200 calories of food intake – and minimal nutrition — that agricultural economists and the UN take to be the survival norm appropriately averaged across age groups, locations and kinds of labour) at least the additional 450-500 million who would be living in the Rs. 45-90 a day range would be well out of poverty. In fact, a substantial proportion of the people living under the lower poverty line would be out of poverty too. There might perhaps remain some 50 to 100 million poor, malnourished Indians whose long-term welfare could easily be looked after by the prosperity all around.

Not only would Indian politicians, government officials, businessmen and their consultants be jumping out of their seats in sheer disbelief that their superpower fantasies may actually be realised, but if this state of affairs was representative of the impoverished world as a whole, the World Bank would be out of business, their achieved goal of a "world free of poverty" having ironically led them there!

Sadly, the reality is closer to "a world free of the poor". Thanks to the subtleties of PPP calculations it may quite possibly be the case that the number of people across the world who are not able to meet the minimum standards for adequate nutrition is anywhere from 3 to 4 billion, rather than the officially estimated 2.7 billion who are estimated to be living under $2 a day. No one really knows. In other words, we could all be off by a whole continent!

Some experts in the field, such as Sanjay Reddy of Columbia University or Robert Wade of the London School of Economics advise deep scepticism about prevailing official estimates, especially of alleged changes thereof on account of globalisation. Wade advocates that "the political economy of statistics" is crucial and argues for greater competition in the market for the generation of international poverty data, so far a *de facto* monopoly of the World Bank. No free market there! There is intense debate among economists and policymakers as to just how much poverty there is in the world and whether it is going up or down with globalisation. According to one expert Angus Deaton, "It seems impossible to make statements about changes in world poverty when the ground underneath one's feet is changing in this way."

Where do the World Bank experts go wrong? A few of them are even known to this writer, and are reliable people of otherwise unimpeachable integrity. Being a dropout economist the author himself appreciates the trials and tribulations of the economists and statisticians at the World Bank who compute the numbers on poverty. They must negotiate a harrowing minefield of data on a daily basis in order to arrive at the sort of numbers the world and its policymakers are interested in. The challenge of measuring poverty accurately, in a world as diverse, complex and dynamic as ours, is immense. But after decades of effort by trained statisticians it should have become possible by now to arrive at somewhat reliable numbers.

The problem is, at bottom, political, rather than one of expertise. The very fact that when making comparisons between enriched and impoverished countries, all monetary magnitudes have to be inflated significantly to get a sense of real values in the poor world, should have been a matter of great ethical concern to economists, something to make them wonder as to how things got to this point. In a world of markets stretched across mountainously uneven playing fields, pricing is determined not so much by the real costs (to human labour and to nature) incurred but by historically determined economic forces like the willingness and ability to pay. Typically, the latter are shaped in profound ways by legacies of inequalities in wealth and power which mainstream economists are trained to avoid taking into account while preparing their advocacy of "free" markets. In the real world, as against the general equilibrium models microeconomists are schooled in, few things are as politically shaped and formed as the structure of relative prices. In particular, the price of labour—wages—is almost entirely a matter of bargaining, as also, we are realising, the price of utilising nature.

Moreover, in our increasingly packaged consumerist world, even global poverty figures must ultimately arrive in a wrapping that is not unpalatably unattractive to the public. Trickle-down will ultimately work, we are repeatedly assured by growth economists. But as the late John Kenneth Galbraith is said to have remarked acerbically, faith in trickle-down is a bit like feeding race horses superior oats so that starving sparrows can forage in their dung. All indications, especially in parts of the world like rural India, are that a decade-and-a-half of corporate globalisation has left undernutrition and malnutrition all but intact, and might quite possibly have worsened the predicament for many millions.

Numbed by the Numbers

In a world brought up to regard numerical precision as a sign of scientific rigour, it is easily forgotten (especially by mainstream economists) that poverty is not merely a matter of numbers. Numbers can only tell us about what the experts call "income poverty". Modern standards of living involve large amounts of intangibles and social consumption, known to economists as "public goods": drinking water, public sanitation, health and education are only some of the services which people in rich countries take for granted because they have been traditionally guaranteed by the State (though in recent years private corporations have queued up, often successfully – especially in impoverished countries – to take control and possession of these services). When these are taken into account it becomes clear that what the experts call the "poverty line" is actually more accurately labeled "starvation line", as some people will have it. Many Indian economists have been advocating a serious upward revision of the poverty line in order to get a better grasp of the economic reality.

Economists have tried to remedy the situation by evolving during the last few decades the Human Development Index (HDI), calculated and issued by the UNDP every year. It tries to take into account life expectancy (as an indicator of health) and levels of adult literacy and enrolment (as indicators of education), apart from considering per capita incomes. It is certainly an improvement over raw numbers for poverty. And yet, if India's HDI is 0.63 and Norway's is 0.96, busy eyes will be tempted to conclude that Norwegians live only one-and-a-half times as well as Indians! The crushing quality of human poverty in a cruel world simply cannot be captured by numbers like this. Nor can the enormity of the environmental damage from deregulated industrial growth be captured, as the World Bank tries to do, in its *Little Green Data Book*, by just offering estimates of greenhouse gas emissions, depletion of forest cover and a few other measurable magnitudes. The effects of runaway industrial growth – the damage done to climatic balances for instance – on the ecosystem are possible to observe now, but not as easily quantified. There are exponential and synergetic changes taking place – for the worse – which might take the best-informed experts by surprise.

Perhaps we would do well to remember Einstein's counsel: "Everything that can be counted does not necessarily count; everything that counts cannot necessarily be counted." The poverty measurement industry loses much sleep and sweat over details that do not matter much. The big picture, perhaps unsurprisingly, is inaccurately reported. The propaganda efforts of governments and corporations succeed in the end in keeping some of the more terrible effects of prevailing economic policies from clear public view, undermining democratic transparency and potential accountability.

Rather than get drowned in swirling oceans of data, we might look for the prominent ridges on the gyrating currents of the monetised economy. However, it is then important to locate them precisely and, crucially, label and flag them accurately. Busy readers don't have time to interpret the fine print. And public patience with economists wears thin.

We only count and measure what is useful, important or interesting. By measuring we indicate that we care about what is measured. The score on poverty, especially if it is shameful, is worth keeping, if only to remind us of the extent of the failure of globalisation not merely to change the lives of the poor but perhaps in turning them for the worse. (If China has lifted tens of millions of families out of poverty, the secret of their success lies in the years and decades preceding globalisation – in the early-1980s rural reforms were carried out, among other things, granting access to land to the rural poor. Besides, the strong foundations of the social infrastructure – education and health – were laid down in the era of communism. Globalisation has only allowed the country to reap the harvest of pre-existing investments better.)

If global poverty statistics are not disseminated accurately, the facts on the ground will only get worse – thanks to misinformed policymaking among other things – and will one day command dreadful obedience from one and all. The rulers of the day risk the implications of Colin Powell's *faux pas* a few years back — of boasting that the number of dead Iraqi civilians did not interest him very much. And the potential consequences across the globe could be as catastrophic as what Iraq is experiencing today.

Poverty and India's Changing Image*

2

C.P. Ravindranathan

There are dismal statistics about poverty in this fourth largest economy in the world, which ranks 126th out of 177 in the World Human Development Index. The need to improve the situation is urgent.

In his Republic Day message, the then President, Mr A.P.J. Abdul Kalam, summed up the outlook for the nation in these words: "If we perform in an integrated way with development politics as the focus, in mission mode with transparency, I visualise even before 2020 that a prosperous nation is possible." His emphasis on the focal nature of development politics aptly captured the vision that should inspire the national effort. A vision that no doubt draws confidence from our achievements so far but is aware of the unfinished tasks that lie ahead.

Reforms

In this season for heady predictions about India's economic prospects in various timeframes, the mention of unfinished tasks would make many people think of the remaining agenda of reforms. But identifying the real unfinished tasks against those which cast an enchantment over us in our quest for double-digit growth, is to get the India story right. All the more so as the country is now moving into the Eleventh Plan. The 56th year of this unique Indian enterprise is an appropriate moment to

---

* *Courtesy*: Hindu Business Line and www.blonnet.com

reflect on what characterises Indian economy beyond the glamour of our achievements in several fields.

Centre Stage in Davos

The glamour was most in evidence at Davos meet. Media reports of the event spoke of India, along with China, assuming centre stage in the global review of economic developments and future growth prospects. With growth rates trending towards 9 per cent and FDI flows surging to $12 billion during 2006-07, India received wide attention at the Davos jamboree, whether from governments, multinational corporations or the international investment community.

And close on its heels, striking a high point in the emergence of Indian multinationals, has come the acquisition of Corus by Tata Steel. More such foreign acquisitions have been foreshadowed, the creditworthiness of Indian companies and India's own upwardly revised country ratings making them favoured clients in the global financial markets for loans and leveraged transactions. Apart from large-scale acquisitions, there is a long train of strategic buy-outs by Indian manufacturing and services companies that are in the offing, with sizeable potential to augment the capabilities and geographical reach of Indian business and industry.

And in the economy, indicators have never been more reassuring than at the present moment. Nowhere is the buoyancy manifested more than in export trade that is now benefiting increasingly from the new capacities created since the commencement of reforms in 1991.

Over the last three years, India's exports have almost doubled. And in the area of information technology and BPO, where its outstanding performance has given the country its high global visibility, the latest Nasscom forecast is $31 billion for the year 2007-08. Manufacturing industry may not reveal such spectacular pace of growth but segments such as automobiles and two-wheelers measure up to the Chinese benchmarks.

What is perhaps as important as all these impressive developments in the Indian economy is the vastly changed perception of India's prospects as a market and production base on the part of global business and industry as well as of governments and opinion-makers in industrial nations. Leading figures of MNCs, such as those of IBM, Microsoft, GE and Wal-Mart, are among those who have hailed the possibilities for India. The increasing coverage that Indian companies are now receiving in the world economic press is an indication of the perceived change of regard that it has for India's capability to perform and compete effectively in a globalised economy.

While the Indian story can thus be expected to engage world attention even as the Chinese story bids fairly well to dominate, there is one significant difference between the two—a difference both in substance and resonance. That difference turns on the one dominant Indian reality that is almost a defining element for the country in the eyes of the world.

In simple terms, while both China and India are poor developing countries by accepted criteria, China has made far greater strides in elimination of poverty, compared to India. Statistics of per capita income and other details apart, poverty is no longer a visible feature in China the way it continues to be in India.

And in the imagination of the wide world, China has virtually ceased to be a poor country; it is rather a fast-growing premier emerging nation with increasing dominance in international trade and production and a formidable competitor in metrics of economic prowess with the leading industrial nations.

Dismal Poverty Statistics

The pathos of the Indian story is that 220-230 million of our people, that is 22 per cent of the total population, are poor, according to the latest findings of the National Sample Survey. That makes India home to the world's largest proportion of the poor, even if the percentage of people living below the poverty line reduced from 36 per cent in 1993-94 to 22 per cent in 2004-05.

There are other dismal statistics about poverty in this fourth largest economy in the world (by GDP at purchasing power parity): 126th rank out of 177 in the World Human Development

Index and the rate of child malnutrition double that of sub-Saharan Africa. With such factual and visible evidence reinforcing existing bias, the defining element of our economy would remain identified with our poor millions, much as we would like it to be otherwise.

The painful paradox of such poverty in the midst of consistently high rates of economic growth over the last few years and the sustained development effort pursued through economic planning since 1950 is the measure of the pathos in the Indian story.

What is all the more disquieting is that there has been no dearth of recognition in political rhetoric or official thinking of the need for elimination of poverty as the primary objective for the country but what has been done and accomplished has fallen so tragically short of proclaimed intentions.

'Direct Attack'

Garibi Hatao of 1971 apart, the Planning Commission itself had said in its approach paper to the Fifth Plan, "The elimination of abject poverty will not be attained as a corollary to a certain acceleration in the rate of growth of the economy alone. It will be necessary to launch a direct attack on the problems of unemployment, underemployment and massive low-end poverty."

Thirty-six years since that urgent call for action was made, it would be interesting to see what the Planning Commission will have by way of a composite strategy in the Eleventh Plan to deal with poverty in the world's fourth largest economy and how the political class will set about "performing in an integrated way with development politics as the focus".

The government's eight flagship programmes, notably the Rural Employment Guarantee Scheme, are at the heart of the present development effort and each of them requires a rigorous and continuous outcome-based review.

Prices and Poverty in India*

3

Angus Deaton and *Alessandro Tarozzi*

Introduction

In India, as in other countries, indexes of consumer prices perform many important functions. Millions of workers have their wages indexed to some measure of the price level. Just as important is the issue that is our main focus here, the estimation of poverty. Indian poverty rates are defined as the fractions of people living in households whose real per capita total expenditure falls below the poverty line. Data on total expenditures are collected by the National Sample Survey (NSS) in money terms so that, for each new round of data, the real poverty line must be converted to current rupees by multiplying by an index of prices. Inaccuracy in the estimation of the index, for example, overestimation of the price increase relative to the base, will result in corresponding inaccuracy of the poverty estimates, for example, an underestimation in the rate of poverty reduction. At a time when the data show historically high rates of GDP growth without much reduction in poverty, especially rural poverty, it is important to establish the accuracy of the price and poverty calculations.

The measurement of inflation is not the only role of price indexes in measuring poverty in India. Price indexes are required, not only to establish the rates of inflation in the urban and rural sector of each state, but also to compare price levels between them. In a country where many states are larger than

---

* *Courtesy*: The Great Indian Poverty Debate, Macmillan, India

most nations in the world, price indexes are needed to make comparisons between states. Differences in poverty rates between Indian states affect the amounts of transfers from the centre to the states, and influence discussions about poverty reduction strategies among international lenders such as the World Bank. In the broader context, India contributes more people to world poverty than does any other country and changes in the way the Indian poor are counted can have significant effects on the world total.

For purposes of tracking poverty over time, the two most important price indexes in India are the Consumer Price Index for Industrial Workers (CPIIW) and the Consumer Price Index for Agricultural Labourers (CPIAL). Reweighted versions of each are used to update the urban and rural poverty lines. Until it was revised in November 1995, the CPIAL itself was based on prices regularly collected from a sample of 422 villages, weighted using an expenditure pattern that dates back to 1960–61. By the time of the revision in 1995, which was later than any of the survey data used in this paper, the weights for the CPIAL were more than three decades out of date, an unusually long time period for any major price index anywhere in the world.

The CPIIW was revised in October 1988. Prior to that date, the base year was 1960, with weights derived from a survey of workers from 1958–59. Prices were collected from shops in a number of markets in 50 industrial centres throughout India. After October 1988, the weights were updated using a 1981–82 survey, with a new basis in 1982, some old centres were dropped and some new ones added, and the total rose to 70. For both indexes, and in order to maximize comparability over time, the specifications of items priced, the units, the shops, the markets, and the day and the time of the visits were held fixed throughout the life of the series. To the extent that there are problems with these price series, they are likely to come from the unusually long periods between revisions. Not only are the weights of these Laspeyres indexes long out of date by the time of transition, but there must also be concern about the continued representativeness of the villages, centres, and markets over such long periods. Whether or not the price indexes are seriously affected is ultimately an empirical question, though it is often supposed (for example in the comparable debate over the CPI in the United States) that Laspeyres indexes will increasingly overstate inflation as the base period recedes into the past, a tendency that will be exacerbated by the failure to pick up new goods (whose prices are often falling rapidly) and discard old (whose prices may be stagnant or even rising).

For the purposes of updating the official poverty lines used by the Planning Commission, the CPIAL and CPIIW are reweighted using national level consumption patterns of people around the poverty line in 1973–74. The primitive price data are the same as for the CPIAL and CPIIW themselves, but the commodity level prices are weighted using the more recent (although still elderly by world standards) and more poverty-relevant weights. These indexes are clearly superior to the CPIAL and CPIIW themselves for the purposes of the poverty calculations, but they also inherit any deficiencies in the underlying prices.

The purpose of this paper is to provide an independent set of calculations of Indian price indexes using data for two year-long periods, 1987–88, and 1993–94, periods that are the same as those for the last two official poverty calculations. We provide estimates of the rate of inflation over the six year period for All India and for 17 of the largest states, by sector, plus Delhi. We also provide separate price indexes for the rural and urban sectors for each of the 17 states and for All India in both periods, as well as estimates of price levels across states by sector in each of the two periods. The sources of data for both prices and expenditure patterns are the 43rd and 50th rounds of the NSS, both of which collected extensive data on consumption of individual items. The use of expenditure surveys to calculate weights for consumer price indexes is standard practice throughout the world. The innovation here is the use of information from the surveys on the prices themselves. For most of the commodities in the NSS surveys, respondents are asked to provide information on how much they spent on the item and on the physical quantity purchased, for example 8 rupees on 2 kilos of rice. The ratio of expenditure to volume provides a measure of price, or more precisely, a measure of unit value.

Compared with the use of the CPIAL and CPIIW, this approach has both advantages and disadvantages. One strength is the size of the samples involved and their representativeness across states and sectors. More than 3.5 million pairs of expenditures and quantities are sampled in each of the two rounds, and the NSS samples are designed to be representative at the state and sector level (and indeed beyond). In consequence, it is possible to construct, not only price indexes that track inflation over time, but also price indexes that compare price levels across states and sectors. A second advantage of unit values is that they relate to actual transactions, not to prices listed or reported by shops. Third, because the transactions are linked to the people who made them, it is possible to stratify prices and price indexes by socio-economic characteristics, such as level of living, or occupation, or demographic structure.

There are two main disadvantages to the use of unit values. Not all goods and services have readily defined quantities. In particular, while unit values are available for most foods, for alcohol and tobacco, and for fuels, they are not collected for such items as transportation or housing. In India, the covered goods comprise between two-thirds and three-quarters of the budget, which makes the exercise worth doing, but which would obviously not be the case in a country such as the United States. Even so, when using price indexes constructed from unit values, it is always important to keep in mind the likely effects of the excluded categories, and in particular the effects on comparisons between urban and rural sectors of omitting the prices of housing and of transportation.

The second disadvantage is that unit values are not prices. Even when goods are defined at the maximum feasible level of disaggregation, many goods are not perfectly homogeneous, so that any given unit value will reflect, not only price, but the mix of varieties within the category. As a result, unit values differ from one purchaser to another in a way that is not caused by differences in prices. In particular, richer households have higher unit values than poorer households, a fact that has been used to study the choice of quality since Prais and Houtkakker (1955), see Deaton (1988, 1997, Chapter 5) for modern treatments. The quality problem can be dealt with in part by disaggregating to the maximum extent permitted by the data. In the analysis below, we work with more than two hundred items of expenditure. Even so, the literature shows that the total expenditure elasticity of unit values is small, even for fairly broad aggregates of goods—such as "cereals" or "pulses". Beyond that, it is important to inspect the data on unit values and to document their price-like characteristics, for example that in a given round and state that a large number of people report the same unit value, and that the unit values have the appropriate patterns of variation over regions and seasons of the year.

The rest of this paper is organized as follows. In Section 1 below, we explain how the unit values and expenditure weights are calculated from the detailed survey data, and we provide summaries of the results and of the methods used to obtain them. Because there are so many observations, more than 7 million unit values, and because each must be examined before being incorporated into the price indexes, the data processing stage of this work has been both long and complex. Nevertheless, we have tried to provide enough detail to permit replication of our results, and our STATA code is available on request. Section 2 is also methodological, and presents the index number formulas used in the calculations, as well as the strengths and weaknesses of each. It also explains why some of the indexes are much more difficult to calculate than others, in particular, why the interstate comparisons of prices are likely to be much less reliable than comparisons over time, with comparisons between urban and rural prices somewhere in between. Section 3 presents the main results and compares the price index numbers calculated here with the two official price indexes. Section 4 considers the implications for the calculations of poverty rates between 1987–88 and 1993–94, as well as for the 1993–94 rates themselves under alternative assumptions about interstate and intersector price variation. Section 5 offers some tentative conclusions, as well as an outline of the work that remains to be done.

Section 1: Using the NSS Data to Calculate Unit Values and Expenditure Patterns

The NSS samples from the 43rd and the 50th Rounds are described in Table 3.1 which shows the distribution of sample households over states and sectors, as well as the total number of purchases recorded for the food, alcohol and tobacco, and fuel categories, the 228 detailed components of which are listed in Table 3.1A. Table 3.1 lists information for All India, which is the complete sample, and for the 17 largest states plus Delhi; clearly it is only for urban Delhi that there are a significant number of sample households. There are 128,101 sample households in the 43rd Round and 115,354 in the 50th Round. By dividing the "purchases" column by the "households" column, we see that, on average, urban households, who have access to a wider range of goods and are typically better off than rural households, record expenditure on around 40 of the items used here, while rural households reported purchases of about 30 items. In total, over the two surveys, there are 8.3 million quantity/expenditure pairs available for analysis; as we shall see below, this number will be reduced somewhat as we proceed.

For each item of expenditure, household respondents are asked to report both the quantity and value of purchases over the last 30 days. The NSS records expenditures in considerable detail which is shown (for the goods used here and for the 50th Round) in Table 3.1A. The comparable list of goods for the 43rd Round is almost identical apart from the important difference that goods bought from the public distribution system (PDS in the Table) are recorded separately from goods from other sources in the 50th Round but not in the 43rd. We have made no attempt to work with the data on clothing and footwear, where there is also some information on quantities purchased, e.g. dhotis and sarees in meters, or shoes in pairs.

For a few of the commodities listed in Table 3.1A, it is effectively impossible to measure quantities, and the questionnaire does not attempt to do so. These commodities (or commodity groups) are therefore dropped from the analysis. They are as follows: egg products, other fresh fruits, other beverages (Horlicks, etc.), biscuits and confectionery, salted refreshments, prepared sweets, other processed food, other drugs and intoxicants, dung cakes, gobar gas, and other fuel and light. Several of these fall into the "other" or residual category within a larger group; for example, other drugs and intoxicants is the residual category in a group that contains toddy, beer, liquor, ganja, and opium. As we shall see later, not only these but several other residual categories do not have well-defined units. There are also few cases where the units change between the two rounds. For example, lemons (guavas) were measured in kilograms (units) in the 43rd Round and in units (kilograms) in the 50th Round. We retain such items for comparisons between states or sectors within each round but, since we have no way of knowing how many lemons or guavas are in a kilo, we drop them when making comparisons between the two rounds.

For each consumption record, a unit value was calculated by dividing expenditure by quantity. The NSS collects data separately for commodities purchased in the market, for commodities produced or grown at home, and for commodities obtained as gifts or loans. Unit values were calculated by dividing the sum of the three kinds of expenditure by the sum of the three kinds of quantity. This procedure effectively weights each of three possible unit values by the shares of expenditure devoted to each. Working commodity by commodity, the unit values were then checked for plausibility as indicators of price. There is no foolproof way of doing this. Nevertheless, there are a number of obvious problems to guard against, and procedures can be developed to detect them. One such is the difficulty of defining units for physical quantities. Expenditures are always measured in rupees, and the concept and its units are clear. For quantities, there is sometimes a choice of units; for example, items can be bought one by one, or by weight. There are also local variations in units, so that what works in one place may not work as well somewhere else. Some customary units are not well-defined in terms of weight; goods bought by the bunch, box, bag, or packet will be converted by the respondent or the enumerator, but the conversion may be less than accurate. To the extent that errors are made—eggs measured in units for some households, and in dozens for others—the unit values will have multi-modal distributions, with peaks corresponding to each distinct unit.

A second problem, which can also be detected by looking for multiple modes, is when two or more distinct goods are included within a single commodity. For example, if milk (liquid) and milk products (expensive sweets) are lumped together, the unit values will cluster around the milk price and the sweet price. While gross contamination is avoided by using the maximal detail, inspection of Table 3.1A shows that, even with so many items, there is still room for heterogeneity within many of the categories. If the compounded goods are sufficiently similar, the unit value may still give a useful indication of prices. The problem arises when there are spatial or temporal differences in the mixture, so that a compound of (cheap) A and (expensive) B is primarily A in state 1, but is primarily B in state 2.

Our procedures are part graphical, and part automatic. For each commodity, we draw histograms and one-way plots of the logarithms of the unit values, using each to detect the presence of gross outliers for further investigation. In some cases, outliers are isolated cases that result from errors of misreporting, miscoding, or misinterpretation of units, and are deleted. In other cases, a problem with units or with contamination can be identified and corrected. An automatic method for outlier detection was also used, and unit values eliminated whose logarithms lie more than 2.5 standard deviations from the mean of logarithms. Note that this does not remove the need for the graphical inspection, since gross bimodality would not necessarily be detected by the standard deviation rule. Log unit values were also inspected for plausibility after deletion of outliers. The resulting distributions of unit values were also examined to assess how many purchases clustered at the median—if the unit values are close to being prices, we would expect substantial such clustering—and tested using analysis of variance for cluster (PSU), district, and subround (seasonal effects)—which should be present if variation in unit values is dominated by price variation rather than quality effects or product heterogeneity within the commodity group.

The data examination led to the deletion of a number of goods where unit values appeared not to be reliable, or where there were other unsolved problems of interpretation. Tables 3.2A to 3.5A list the goods involved. Table 3.2A lists the goods omitted because the NSS instructions do not call for quantities to be collected; for reasons that we do not understand, quantity data exist for these commodities, but the associated unit values would have been deleted by our inspection procedures in any case. Tables 3.3A and 3.4A list the additional commodities that were excluded from the 43rd and the 50th Rounds respectively. Most of these cases are "other" residual categories within larger subgroups, where the unit values showed dispersion to match the obvious heterogeneity in the definition of the group. Some are goods where there is clear evidence of bimodality (e.g. Liquid Petroleum Gas in the 43rd Round, where there is apparently more than one unit of measurement, but where we were unable to make a suitable correction. There has apparently also been a black market in LPG in India, which may explain the price variation.) One or two of the goods lost (for example, cups of tea and coconuts) are important items in some states, there is no obvious reason for problems, and their loss is unfortunate. Table 3.5A lists the additional commodities that had to be eliminated in the comparisons between rounds, but not within them. In addition to the two goods whose units were changed according to the NSS documentation, there are five other commodities where the distributions of prices in the two rounds are so far apart that it seems likely that an undocumented change of units took place. (For example, coal gas is measured in "standard units" which perhaps changed in the intervening six years.)

Summary unit values were calculated from the "cleaned" data by commodity, by sector, by state, and by round. In addition to the 18 "large" states (as listed in Table 3.1), comparable calculations were made for All India. In preference to means, we use medians for the summary unit values, largely because of their greater resistance to any remaining outliers. The calculations of medians are weighted using the household multipliers supplied by the NSS; since purchases are assumed to be made at the household level, it is appropriate to weight using household weights.

For each household in the surveys, we calculated the share in the budget devoted to each commodity; more precisely, we used the total value of expenditures on the commodity (summing purchases, home production, gifts and loans, and other) divided by household total expenditure on all goods and services, constructed from the NSS–supplied per capita total household expenditure multiplied by household size. These budget shares were then averaged over all households in a given sector, state, and round, using as weights the NSS multipliers multiplied by household size. There are three points to notice about this construction. First, we use means rather than medians; because the budget shares are automatically bounded between zero and one, there is less concern about the effects of an isolated undetected outlier. Second, the weighting scheme, by multiplying by household size, puts the weights on an individual, rather than household, basis. Because individuals—not households—are the appropriate units for welfare analysis, the commodity weights for price indexes, which is what the budget shares will become, are better computed on an individual than a household basis.

Third, the use of averaged budget shares will generate "democratic" price indexes (Prais 1958; Pollak 1991) rather than the "plutocratic" price indexes that are routinely produced by national statistical offices. The weights for the latter are aggregate consumers' expenditure on each commodity divided by the aggregate of consumers' expenditure on all commodities; as is easily shown, this ratio of aggregates is the average of the individual household ratios weighted by total household expenditure. As a result, the ratio of aggregates weights rich households more than poor households, hence the label of "plutocratic". Plutocratic indexes are not well suited for calculating the cost-of-living for poor people. Ideally, we might wish to use price indexes whose weights are tailored to the expenditure patterns of those below the poverty line, and it would be straightforward to do so using the NSS data. However, because Indian poverty lines are typically around the middle of the per capita expenditure distribution, democratic indexes will not differ much from poverty-line weighted indexes. Checking this conjecture is an important topic for further research.

There is also a (minor) data problem associated with the construction of the budget shares. In the 43rd Round, there are six pairs of commodity items (jowar and jowar products, bajra and bajra products, maize and maize products, barley and barley products, small millets and small millets products, and ragi and ragi products) where some expenditures are entered under one member of the pair, and some under another, so that it is only possible to work with the pair as a combined category, rather than with each separately. For each of these pairs, we work with the budget share of the two together, and with the unit value of the first. This appears to give sensible results.

Table 3.2 shows an illustrative selection of results, for thirteen commodities for the rural sectors of Uttar Pradesh and Kerala in the two rounds. These two states were chosen because their expenditure patterns are very different. Since it is clearly impossible to show all the commodities, we have selected for each case the thirteen most important defined by the size of their average budget shares. Clearly, which commodities have the largest budget share is neither robust to the degree of disaggregation nor to the definition of commodities, and we claim no significance for our choice other than that the goods are ones purchased by large numbers of households. The Table lists the commodity names, the units in which they are measured, the mean of their budget share over all households, the number of households recorded as making purchases of each, and the number of households deleted by the outlier elimination procedures. Finally, the last column in each panel shows the median unit values reported. A number of points should be noted.

The most important single item in all four tables is the main staple, atta in UP, and rice in Kerala, followed by milk, cooking oil, and firewood. In Kerala, the PDS is an important source of rice; in 1993–94, 44 per cent of rice expenditure was in PDS stores. Since rice from these stores was cheaper than rice purchased from other sources, more than half of rice by quantity came through the public system. Some atta in UP is also sold through the PDS, but the amounts are not important enough to show up in the table. (Note that PDS and other sources are not separated in the 43rd Round, so that the bottom panel shows combined budget shares. Hence the 20.6 budget share of rice in Kerala in the 43rd Round should be compared with 10.8 plus 8.6 (19.6) per cent in the 50th Round.)

The differences in the consumption patterns across the two states highlight the difficulty of making interstate price comparisons, as we shall see in more detail in Section 3 below. If we are to compare the price level in Kerala with the price level in UP, we will need to price atta in Kerala, which comprises more than 14 per cent of the budget in UP, but which is rarely bought in Kerala, and whose price is irrelevant for most of its inhabitants. Similar issues arise for fresh fish, coconuts, and for coconut versus mustard oil. These differences of consumption patterns pose familiar problems for analysts of price indexes, although more usually for price comparisons between countries, not within them.

The Table also shows that the number of outliers is small relative to the numbers of original purchases in the data. Note also that the median unit values are often whole numbers. Large numbers of purchases take place at or close to the numbers shown. For example, in UP in the 43rd Round (bottom left panel of the Table) 1,706 of the 4,862 recorded purchases of atta (or more than a third of total purchases when weighted) were at exactly 2 rupees per kilo. More than half of purchases of liquid milk were at 4 rupees per liter, and although only 10 per cent of purchases of mustard oil were at exactly 26 rupees, more than a half took place within 10 per cent of 26 rupees.

Although it is difficult to use Table 3.2 to get an informal idea of price differences between Kerala and UP, it is straightforward to see the effects of inflation and to guess its extent. For many of the goods shown, prices in 1993–94 were between one and a half and twice their levels in 1987–8. The relative ease of making intertemporal compared with spatial comparisons of prices will carry through to the more formal results in Section 3, where the estimates of price inflation will be more robust than the estimates of price differences across states or sectors.

Section 2: Alternative Price Indexes: Theory

When price indexes are used to make comparisons over time, it is often the case that neither relative prices nor patterns of expenditure change very much between the two dates in the comparison. In such cases, different price indexes tend to look quite similar, and the choice of index is not of great importance. We shall see that this is the case here for comparisons of given sectors of given states between the two rounds. But relative prices and expenditure patterns are very different between states, and to a lesser extent between sectors within states, so that the precise choice of index is often important for these comparisons. In the calculations below, we work with four different indexes that are briefly presented and discussed here.

The Laspeyres index compares prices in period (state, sector) 1 with a base period (state, sector) 0 according to the formula

$$P_{10}^{L} = \sum_{k=1}^{n} q_{0k}p_{1k} \Big/ \sum_{k=1}^{n} q_{0k}p_{0k} \tag{1}$$

where q's are quantities and p's are prices, where the first suffix on prices and quantities refers to the location (place) of the price, either base 0 or comparison 1, and the second suffix k refers to the commodity and runs over all n goods. The Paasche price index is written

$$P_{10}^{L} = \sum_{k=1}^{n} q_{1k}p_{1k} \Big/ \sum_{k=1}^{n} q_{1k}p_{0k} \tag{2}$$

For the purposes of the calculations of this paper, it is more convenient to write these indexes in terms of budget shares and price relatives. The budget share of good i in location 0 (say) is defined as

$$w_{0i} = q_{0i}p_{0i} \Big/ \sum_{k=1}^{n} p_{0k}q_{0k} \tag{3}$$

These budget shares will be taken to be the (weighted) average of the comparable budget shares over all households in the state, sector, and round under consideration. By rearranging (1) and (2), we can easily show that

$$P_{10}^{L} = \sum_{k=1}^{n} w_{0k}\left(\frac{p_{1k}}{p_{0k}}\right) \tag{4}$$

while the Paasche index takes the form

$$P_{10}^{P} = \left[\sum_{k=1}^{n} w_{1k}\left(\frac{p_{1k}}{p_{0k}}\right)^{-1}\right]^{-1} \tag{5}$$

In both cases, the price relatives of the individual goods convey the price information, and the budget shares provide the weights, the base period for the Laspeyres and the comparison period for the Paasche.

Neither the Laspeyres nor the Paasche is particularly suitable for making comparisons between Indian states. As we saw in Section 1 using the illustrative comparison between Kerala and UP, consumption patterns different greatly across states even to the extent that a staple in one state may not be consumed at all in another. In consequence, prices for the staple in the "wrong" state are either not observed at all, or at best will be poorly measured. For example, for the 43rd Round, Table 3.2 shows that 4,862 rural households in UP bought atta, but only 272 rural households in Kerala did so. Coconut oil, purchased by 2,354 households in rural Kerala, was purchased by only 5 households in UP. And even if the prices are available, and can be accurately measured, it is not clear that the price of coconut oil in UP, where people use mustard oil for cooking, is really relevant to calculations of the standard living. The usual way of thinking about this problem is to note that neither Laspeyres nor Paasche indexes do an adequate job of capturing consumer substitution, that when faced with differences in relative prices, consumers are likely to adjust their consumption patterns towards relatively cheap goods, and away from relatively more expensive ones. Of course, it also might be argued that the difference between UP and Kerala is not merely a difference in relative prices, but a difference in tastes or if not in tastes, in the environment, including not only the physical environment but such things as provision of public goods. If so, it is not clear that there exists any satisfactory basis for comparing price levels between them.

As noted long ago, the geometric mean of the Paasche and the Laspeyres, the Fisher Ideal Index, does a better job than either one in capturing substitution. The Fisher index is defined as

$$P_{10}^{F} = \sqrt{P_{10}^{L}\, P_{10}^{P}} \tag{6}$$

We shall also use the Törnqvist price index, which is defined by

$$\text{In } P_{10}^{T} = \sum_{k=1}^{n} \frac{w_{1k} + w_{0k}}{2} \text{ In}\left(\frac{p_{1k}}{p_{0k}}\right) \tag{7}$$

Because both the Fisher and the Törnqvist indexes use both sets of budget shares, they mute the negative effects of using one or other (the budget share of atta in UP to measure prices in Kerala, or the budget share of coconut oil to measure prices in UP). More generally, both Törnqvist and Fisher Ideal indexes are superlative indexes, Diewert (1976), which means that they are exactly equal to a true cost-of-living index number for some utility-based demand system that is general enough to provide a second-order approximation to preferences, or a first-order approximation to the demand system. It should be noted that superlative indexes deal with substitution effects better than they deal with income effects. Superlative indexes are only exact in the case of homothetic preferences (preferences not only have to be the same in Kerala and UP, but expenditure patterns in both should not vary with the level of living), and when homotheticity is violated, offer an approximation only at some level of living intermediate between the two points being compared. It is not clear how this intermediate point should be interpreted, nor whether the superlative indexes answer the questions to which we most want answers. Even so, it is clear that, for comparisons between states and between sectors within states, it makes more sense to use Törnqvist or Fisher indexes than Paasche or Laspeyres.

Note that the Törnqvist and Fisher indexes have another advantage, which is that they satisfy the "reversal" test. If prices are (say) ten per cent higher in UP than Kerala, or more precisely, if the price index for UP relative to Kerala is 110, then prices are ten per cent lower in Kerala than in UP (or the price index for Kerala relative to UP is 100/110 = 90.9). Because of the change in weights as we move from one base to another, neither Laspeyres nor Paasche index has this property. Since the "reversal" property is so deeply ingrained in the way that we talk about prices, there is much to be said for index numbers that embody it.

Another, perhaps equally appealing, property is not satisfied by these index numbers. This is the "circularity" or "transitivity" property. Suppose that we have three situations, A, B, and C. We can calculate an index for B relative to A, and for C relative to B. If these are multiplied together, we get an "indirect" price index for C relative to A, in contrast to the "direct" estimate that comes from comparing C with A in one step. Circularity is satisfied if these two indexes are the same. The failure of this property arises in the current context when we wish to combine urban to rural price indexes with state to All India indexes. Suppose, for example, that in the rural sector, UP has an index of 110 relative to 100 for All India, while in the urban sector, UP is 105 relative to 100 for All India. If the All India urban to rural price index is 115 (say), then the "indirect" route gives us an urban to rural price index for UP of 120.75 (115 × 105) to 110 (110 × 100) or 109.8. But we can also use the "direct" route to compare urban and rural prices in UP and there is no guarantee that we will get the same answer. As we shall see, this sort of "circularity" failure has caused problems in context of measuring poverty in India.

Section 3: Price Indexes: Results

Table 3.3 shows the results of possibly the greatest interest, the comparison of price levels between the two rounds, by state, and by sector. Following a format that will be applied in all the tables in this section, we show first the total share of the budget covered by all of the goods that go into the price indexes, averaged over all households included. The closer these numbers to unity, the more complete the price index. Since the various price indexes involve two sets of budget shares, the "base" and the "comparison," there are generally two sets of budget shares in the tables. We then present the four price indexes, Laspeyres, Paasche, Fisher Ideal, and Törnqvist. In most cases, the last two indexes are very close to one another, and since both have the "superlative" index property, they are our preferred estimates. In all cases, the code is written so as to exclude any good from the price indexes when in either base or comparison data set, there are less than 20 observations on its price. Although the choice of 20 is arbitrary, the results are not sensitive to reasonable variations, and some such rule is required to eliminate cases where there are only one or two observations on a given price.

Table 3.3 shows that, for All India, goods comprising 74.6 per cent of the budget were included in the rural sector of the 43rd Round, falling to 70.7 per cent in the 50th Round. This decline is to be expected from Engel's Law if there is an increase in real incomes, and would be interpreted by some as evidence that real incomes have indeed been increasing. The shares covered are lower in the urban sector, 67.6 and 63.4 per cent, which is again to be expected if urban areas are somewhat better off, and because of the relatively greater importance for urban consumers of items such as housing and transportation. With a few exceptions, these patterns of shares between the rounds and between urban and rural sectors are replicated across the individual states shown in the Table. In the rural sector, the covered share rose in only three states, Haryana, Himachal Pradesh, and Punjab, and in the urban sector, increased only in Delhi (where the covered share is lower than anywhere else). Several states, particularly in urban sectors, show large decreases in the covered share. In the rural sector, Gujarat, Karnataka,

Madhya Pradesh, and Maharashtra showed declines of more than 5 percentage points, while the same occurred in the urban sectors of Assam, Gujarat, Jammu & Kashmir, Karnataka, Kerala, Madhya Pradesh, and Maharashtra. While the share of the budget devoted to food is far from being an infallible guide to welfare, these results are consistent with an increase in well-being that is somewhat unevenly spread, and that is stronger in urban than rural sectors.

The All India (Törnqvist) price index shows an increase between the rounds of 69.8 per cent for the rural sector, and of 73.8 per cent in the urban areas. The CPIAL, which is the relevant comparison for the rural sector, increased by 76.3 per cent, while the CPIIW, which is the relevant index for urban comparisons, increased by 75.1 per cent. The versions of the CPIAL and CPIIW used in the official poverty lines, and which are calculated by dividing the 50th Round lines by the 43rd Round lines, are shown in the final column. The rural poverty weighted index rose by a little more than the CPIAL, 78.7 per cent, and the urban poverty weighted index by a little less than the CPIIW, 73.5 per cent. The differences between our calculations the "official" numbers are not very large, but the direction of the difference, with the official prices overestimating inflation in the rural sector, appears in many of the entries in the Table. The Laspeyres index estimates more inflation than the two superlative indexes which allow for some substitution; in the urban sector, our All India Laspeyres is identical to the CPIIW while in the rural sector, the Laspeyres takes us only about a third of the way from the superlative indexes to the CPIAL. Across (most but not all of) the states, as for All India, our calculations show more overestimation of inflation in rural than in urban areas, so that recalculations of poverty rates in the next section will show more effect on calculated rural than urban poverty.

One possible reason why our calculations might systematically understate the rate of inflation would be if the rate of inflation of non-covered goods, including housing and transportation, has typically been higher than the rate of inflation of the covered goods. We do not currently have to hand the

CPIAL and CPIIW disaggregated by commodity groupings. However, the Indian Labour Yearbooks show that, for All India, the all-items or general versions of the two price indexes have been rising less rapidly than the food component alone. Hence, if we were to combine our indexes for the covered goods with the relevant components of the CPIAL and CPIIW for the non-covered items, the result would show less inflation than our current estimates. We plan to carry out these calculations on a state by state basis when we have the relevant data.

At the state level, our calculations show less inflation over the period than do the corresponding CPIAL or CPIIW indexes in all the states shown except for rural Jammu & Kashmir, Maharashtra, Orissa, and Tamil Nadu, and for urban Andhra Pradesh, Jammu & Kashmir, and Punjab. (Note that we do not currently have data on the CPIAL for Haryana nor on either the CPIAL nor CPIIW for Himachal Pradesh.) The differences between the two sets of indexes are smaller in the urban areas, and the largest differences occur in the rural areas of a few states, notably Bihar, Kerala, Rajasthan, and Uttar Pradesh. It is worth noting that some of these states have relatively high poverty rates, where a reduction in the price level is likely to have the largest effects.

Indexes for urban prices relative to a rural base are presented in Table 3.4. The choice of which sector to use as base makes a difference to all but the two superlative indexes, although note that the Laspeyres index for rural relative to urban is the reciprocal of the Paasche index for urban relative to rural. For India as a whole, urban prices for covered goods were 11.4 per cent higher than rural prices in the 43rd Round. By the 50th round, this difference had expanded to 15.6 per cent. (Note that this difference is qualitatively consistent with the results in Table 3.3, where the urban rate of inflation was calculated to be somewhat higher than the rural rate.) There is some variation across states in urban–rural price differentials, and these variations seem to be stable over time. Urban Kerala is only slightly more expensive than rural Kerala; the same appears to be the case for Himachal Pradesh and Jammu & Kashmir in 1987–88, though less so in 1993–94. At the other end of the scale, the urban price differential was highest in Uttar Pradesh, West Bengal, Maharashtra, Madhya Pradesh, Punjab, and Haryana.

For many years, until the Expert Group Report of 1993, Indian poverty lines were set (in 1973–84 prices) at Rs. 49 of per capita household expenditure for rural areas and Rs. 57 for urban areas, a difference of 15 per cent. Clearly, our estimates in Table 3.4, particularly for the later round, are consistent with such a difference. Of course, our estimates exclude between a quarter and a third of the budget, including important items like housing and transportation so that a fuller account of the budget would presumably raise the relative cost of living in urban areas. There are no official price indexes for urban to rural differentials. Nevertheless, the Expert Group calculated a set of poverty lines for 1987–88 that differed between urban and rural in each state, and so contained an implicit set of urban to rural price differences. The Planning Commission subsequently adopted a modified version of the Expert Group's proposals so that the official poverty lines also contain a set of implicit urban to rural price ratios and these can be obtained by dividing the urban by the rural lines. These are listed in the penultimate column of Table 3.4, labeled "PL deflators." (That these urban to rural indexes are implicit should be emphasized. The Expert Group did not derive these price deflators from an explicit set of urban to rural price indexes. Instead, they started from the original urban poverty line, and adjusted it by a price index for the urban areas of the different states in Minhas, Jain, Kansal, and Saluja (1988). Similarly, they adjusted the original rural line by the statewise rural price differences from 1960–61 in Chaterjee and Bhattacharyya (1974). The implicit price indexes for urban relative to rural are therefore generated in an indirect manner that did not make them conform to other evidence or that placed limits on their plausibility, something that can be thought of as a failure of the circularity criterion.)

As we might expect, given that the non-covered goods include housing and transportation, the urban–rural price differentials implicit in the poverty lines are always larger than those calculated in this paper. For All India, the "official" urban prices are higher than rural prices by 40.8 per cent, compared with 11.4 per cent for the Törnqvist index, and the official urban premium varies across states from a high of 65.2 per cent in Andhra Pradesh to lows of only 15.3 per cent in West Bengal and is actually negative in Assam. Of course, such variability is not in itself implausible, given the variability in the cost of housing from one place to another. (Even so, it seems surprising that the second lowest differential should be in the state that contains India's largest city.) Another way of comparing our calculations with those of the official indexes is to work out the price index for non-covered goods that would be required to reconcile the two sets of results. We do this by calculating the price relative which, when inserted into a Törnqvist index with the covered goods, would yield a price index equal to the official estimate. These numbers are shown in the last column. For All India, the price of uncovered goods in the urban areas would have to be 2.74 times its level in rural areas, and for individual states, the ratios range from 5.5 in Madhya Pradesh to 1.3 in West Bengal and 0.7 in Assam. It is hard to accept that the high figures are correct, and thence not to conclude that the official urban to rural price differentials are not too large. Indeed, they are sufficiently large as to cause measured poverty rates to be higher in urban than rural areas in several states where many observers have found the finding implausible, for example, in comparison with other non-expenditure-based measures of poverty, such as levels of infant mortality or literacy.

Tables 3.5 and 3.6 present price indexes for differences in prices across states. For the reasons discussed in the theory section, these are the most difficult price indexes to compute, and are likely to be most sensitive to a few outliers, or to the fundamental problems of comparing groups of consumers whose tastes are very different. One symptom of these problems is the sensitivity of these calculations to the precise definition of the index. In these tables, the Paasche and Laspeyres tend to be further apart than in the urban rural or over time comparisons, and even the Törnqvist and Fisher indexes tend not to be the same. Rather than present the complete matrix of state by state comparisons, in which every state acts as a base for every other state, we have selected "All India" as the base, so that we have, as before, one index for each sector of each state. This procedure also has the advantage that the Laspeyres indexes, which price the same bundle in each of the states, are conceptually the same as the state price indexes calculated by the Expert Group. Table 3.5 shows the estimates from the 43rd Round; Table 3.6 those for the 50th Round.

According to these calculations, the differences in aggregate price levels across states are not large, at least not for the covered goods (for the cost of housing, matters may be different). In 1987–88, only rural Gujarat, rural Assam, and rural Tamil Nadu are more than 5 per cent more expensive than All India, and rural Uttar Pradesh, Andhra Pradesh, Madhya Pradesh, and Punjab are more than 5 per cent less expensive. Among the urban areas, only Gujarat and Maharashtra are more than 5 per cent above the All India estimate, and only Andhra Pradesh, Jammu & Kashmir, and Orissa are more than 5 per cent less. By 1993–94, there is somewhat more dispersion in the price indexes. Rural Gujarat and Kerala are 10 per cent more expensive than rural India as a whole, and Assam, Maharashtra, Punjab, Rajasthan, and Tamil Nadu are more than 5 per cent more expensive. Madhya Pradesh, Orissa, and Uttar Pradesh are more than 5 per cent below the average. In the urban sectors, in only Maharashtra the price level is more than 10 per cent above the All India urban average, while Assam, Gujarat, and Delhi are 5 per cent or more above. Andhra Pradesh, Madhya Pradesh, Orissa, and Uttar Pradesh are the states with the lowest urban prices. Nevertheless, it would not be hard to make the case that, given the difficulties of these measurements, and given the lack of evidence for large price differentials, it would be better to ignore interstate price differences in setting poverty lines, if only in the interests of transparency.

Once again, at least for the 43rd Round, it is possible to compare our results with the prices that are implicit in the Planning Commission's poverty lines which in turn derive from the Expert Group report. Dividing each state's official line by the official All India line (within sectors) we can obtain a price index for comparison. The results are listed in the final columns of Tables 3.5 and 3.6. In both sectors, and for both years, these implicit prices are positively correlated with those calculated here, with correlation coefficients between 0.28 and 0.38, but none of these correlations is significantly different from zero. Our own state price relatives are strongly correlated with each other, both over time within sector (correlations greater than 0.7) and within states across sector (correlations again greater than 0.7). This similarity of rural and urban prices across different states is in sharp contrast to the correlations displayed by the official state indexes where the state rural and urban price differentials are negatively correlated across states within each round (correlation –0.40 in the 43rd Round and –0.60 in the 50th). This is in itself a strange result; spatial price differences are moderated by arbitrage, so that prices should be more similar between the urban and rural sectors of the same state than they are across states, precisely the opposite of the pattern in the official lines. The Expert Group statewise price differences, on which the Planning Commission lines are based, are taken from Chaterjee and Bhattacharyya (1974) which were calculated for 1960–61, so that there must be some question about their relevance after more than a quarter of a century, especially given the differential rate of inflation by state even over the relatively short period from 1987–88 to 1993–94 (Table 3.3) and the sizeable differences in our calculated statewise price indexes between Tables 3.5 and 3.6.

Section 4: Consequences for Poverty Measurement

Even given a trial price index, there is no straightforward way to calculate its effect on estimated headcount ratios compared with the price index in current use. The problem lies in the need to choose a base year, and in the arbitrariness of any particular choice. In India, 1973–74 is frequently taken as base, and the poverty lines of 49 (rural) and 57 (urban) rupees per head in 1973–74 prices have nearly always been taken as the base from which different updating schemes start. Following this tradition, the obvious way to assess the effects of different prices on poverty estimates would be to start from the assumption that the price indexes in 1973–74 are correct, and then to calculate new price indexes for subsequent years. If it were the case that a Laspeyres index with fixed base were to slowly come adrift from another (for example superlative) index, then the differences in poverty counts would also drift apart over the years. Armed with all the expenditure surveys since 1973–74, it would be possible in principle to repeat the calculations of this paper, and to carry out the repricing exercise. However, we have so far worked with only two full expenditure surveys, 1987–88 and 1993–94, so that our only estimate of the rate of inflation is between those two years. In consequence, the only feasible calculation of poverty rates is one that takes (at least some of) the 1987–88 rates as correct, and then compares the "official" poverty rates in 1993–94 with those calculated using the different price indexes. From this, we can compare the "official" and "experimental" changes in the headcount ratio from 1987–88 to 1993–94. While this calculation is of considerable interest, and makes a first attempt to answer the question about whether price mismeasurement means that rural poverty is falling more rapidly than officially documented, it is certainly not the only possible answer. With another choice of base year (such as 1973–74), the nominal poverty lines in 1987–88 would be different, and because the effects of poverty lines on poverty counts are not the same at different points in the distribution, the effects on the change in the poverty rates between the two years would also be different, even though the inflation rate between them were the same. The change in poverty rates between any two dates is not a unique function of the change in nominal poverty lines between them, but also depends on the level of the lines.

A further complication is that the general agreement on poverty lines in 1973–74 has largely broken down since the publication of the Expert Group Report, with different analysts updating their lines in different ways, so that there is no obvious starting point for our first survey in 1987–88. We have chosen to start from the most "official" of the lines, which are those used by the Planning Commission, which are modified versions of those put forward by the Expert Group. Given our previous criticism of these lines, this may seem like an odd choice. But any choice is more or less arbitrary, and in the absence of a more thoroughgoing analysis, we prefer to look at the effects of redefinition in the vicinity of lines that are currently in use for policymaking within the Government of India. In any case, in our final recommended estimates presented below, we shall make only minimal use of the 1987–88 lines.

Table 3.7 lists the nominal official poverty lines for the two surveys, the associated headcount ratios, and the change in the headcount ratios over the six year period. The poverty lines are taken from the updates of the Expert Group's recommendations in Government of India (1997). The headcount ratios were calculated using the individual record data from the 43rd and the 50th Round; they are not quite identical to the headcount ratios in GOI (1997) which are based on interpolations but are recognizably calculations of the same thing. Note that the All India poverty estimates are calculated by adding up the estimated numbers of people in poverty in each state (including the small states and territories not listed here), and the All India poverty lines are then derived implicitly as the lines that replicate the All India counts from the state-level calculations. Because of the differences in the method of calculation between Table 3.7 and the Planning Commission, the implicit All India lines, shown here as "All India (2)" are also slightly different from the official ones. The replication in Table 3.7 is important to check that there are no major differences of definition or procedures between the official figures and the experimental ones to be calculated below. In substance, the Table shows the familiar picture of poverty rates falling in urban areas—by 6 percentage points for All India, and much more in some states—but with a much more modest decrease in the rural areas—only 2 percentage points for the country as a whole, and five of the states actually show increases in the rural poverty rate over the period.

Table 3.8 repeats the four official price indexes, the CPIAL and the CPIIW themselves, together with their reweighted versions implicit in the official poverty lines in Table 3.7 and obtained by dividing the 1993–94 lines by the 1987–88 lines. The first two columns show that the reweighting of the CPIAL makes little difference, either state by state, or for the country as a whole; the updating index is very close to the CPIAL. This is what would be expected given the high poverty rates in India. For urban poverty lines, the reweighting appears to induce larger deviations from the CPIIW, particularly in a few states (Assam, Bihar, and Maharashtra). It is not transparent from the information to hand why these differences exist, and why they are larger than for the CPIAL.

Table 3.9 shows our own calculations of poverty rates using the inflation rates between 1987–88 and 1993–94 that were calculated in the earlier sections of this paper and that were reported in Table 3.3. In these first calculations, we are ignoring the other price indexes, those for interstate and intersectoral differentials; we take the 1987–88 official lines for each sector of each state as the base, and apply the Törnqvist inflation factors from column 6 of Table 3.3. In this way, we isolate the effects of the different calculated rates of inflation, leaving the urban-rural and statewise differentials for later.

The Table starts by examining the sensitivity to changes in the poverty lines of the headcount ratios in both rounds. Since the headcount ratio is the distribution function of per capita expenditure evaluated at the poverty line, the derivative of the ratio is the density evaluated at the same point. We have calculated these densities using a kernel smoother with a Gaussian kernel and with a bandwidth chosen according to Silverman's (1983) robust version of the optimal bandwidth. The density at the poverty line, multiplied by the poverty line, shows the derivative of the headcount ratio with respect to the logarithm of the poverty line, and the estimates for the two rounds are reported in the first two columns of the Table. (Note that these two columns can also be interpreted as the derivatives of the poverty rates with respect to mean per capita expenditure holding its distribution constant.)

To interpret the derivatives in the first two columns, note for example that the figure of 0.70 for rural Andhra Pradesh in the 43rd Round shows that a one per cent decrease in the nominal poverty line (or equivalently a one per cent decrease in the price deflator) would cause the headcount ratio to fall by 0.70 percentage points, that is from the calculated headcount ratio of 21.04 per cent to 20.34 per cent. These estimates fall between 0.32 (urban Himachal Pradesh) and 1.11 (rural Assam and Bihar). They are larger the larger is the density of the population at or near the poverty line, so that given where poverty lines lie in the state distributions of per capita expenditure in India, they tend to be larger in the poorer states and smaller in the richer states. In the latter the poor are in the tail of the distribution, so that shifts in the mean have relatively little effect on their numbers, while in the poor states, where the poverty line is near the median, shifts in the line (or in economic growth) have much larger effects on the counts. These numbers should be seen as providing a rough rule of thumb for how much to expect differences in price indexes (or growth rates) to affect the poverty rates.

Column 3 in Table 3.9 shows the difference (in percentage points) between the price indexes calculated in this paper and the change in the official price indexes from 1987–88 to 1993–94, where the official indexes are those implicit in the poverty lines. These figures are simply the difference between the logarithms of column 6 and column 8 in Table 3.3. Again we are looking only at inflation rates, making no correction for the interstate or intersectoral price differences. Column 4 repeats the headcount ratio for 1993–94, as reported in Table 3.7, while column 5 reports what the headcount ratio would be if the nominal poverty lines in 1987–88 were updated, not as in the official lines, but by the Törnqvist price indexes in column 6 of Table 3.3.

The last two columns show the changes in the headcount ratios between the two surveys, by the official counts in column 6, and by our counts in column 7. Although there are some differences on a state by state basis, our results for the urban sector are similar to the official results, and the official decline in the urban poverty rate of –6.01 percentage points is revised only to –5.87 percentage points. The differences are much more important in the rural sector. For All India, the reduction in the poverty rate from 1987–88 to 1993–94 moves from only 2 percentage points in the official counts to more than 6 per cent according to our price indexes. The differences are much larger for some states, particularly Assam, Bihar, Haryana, Himachal Pradesh (where the official very puzzling 14 percentage point rise in poverty is eliminated), Kerala, Madhya Pradesh, Rajasthan, and Uttar Pradesh, and in all these cases the adoption of the new price indexes would cause measured poverty to have fallen more rapidly than in the official counts. These calculations are consistent with the view that, between 1987–88 and 1993–94, there was no great difference in the rates of decline of urban and rural poverty in India.

Table 3.10 explores the effects of modifying the Expert Group lines for the urban-rural and interstate price differentials as measured in this paper. Again, we proceed in a series of steps. Column 1 shows the updated Expert Group headcount ratios for each state (other than Jammu & Kashmir). This column replicates the data from column 4 of Table 3.9. Column 2 of Table 3.10 (labeled "New 1") takes the updated Expert Group lines for the rural sector of each state as correct, but calculates the urban poverty lines by applying the urban-rural Törnqvist price indexes for 1993–94 shown in the bottom panel of Table 3.4. The associated headcount ratios are shown in this column; the top panel is unchanged by construction, but the urban headcount ratios in the bottom panel are often dramatically different from the official ratios. For example, according to these estimates, only 9.6 per cent of people in urban Andhra Pradesh are poor, as opposed to 38.8 per cent in the official estimates. There are similar dramatic declines in measured urban poverty in Gujarat, Karnataka, Madhya Pradesh, Maharashtra, Orissa, and Tamil Nadu, and the All India rate of urban poverty falls from 33 per cent to 19 per cent. But this first step should not be taken too seriously. While it corrects for the almost certainly too large urban-rural price differences in the Expert Group lines, it takes their rural lines as correct, accepting their implicit interstate price differences. The low headcount ratio that we estimate for urban Andhra Pradesh (for example) owes as much to a low starting point in the rural line, as it does to a low price relative from urban to rural.

The next step is taken in column 3, labeled "New 2". These estimates do a more comprehensive job of correcting the official calculations because they correct for state price differences as well as for sector differences. The calculations are done by starting with the (our slightly recalculated version of) official rural poverty line for All India in 1993–94, Rs. 205.67, see Table 3.7. This number is used to generate rural poverty lines for each state by multiplying by the rural Törnqvist price indexes for states relative to All India for 1993–94 shown in the top panel of Table 3.6. The urban lines are then created, state by state, by multiplying by the urban to rural Törnqvist price differentials that are listed in the bottom panel of Table 3.4 (and that were already used in calculating column 2.) Note that the same price indexes could be used differently, converting the All India rural poverty line to an urban poverty line using the All India urban to rural price index, and then applying the state to All India urban price indexes. Because circularity does not hold, the poverty lines derived in this way are different from those actually used, though here the differences are not important.

The "New 2" poverty rates are now slightly higher in the urban areas, though still much less than the official counts. Again, there are large differences for individual states (21 per cent in urban Andhra Pradesh versus 39 per cent, 25 per cent in urban Karnataka versus 40 per cent), and our urban counts are typically lower than the corresponding rural counts. Our price indexes do not support the large interstate or intersectoral differences that are built into the official lines, so that our calculations, unlike the official ones, support the notion that poverty rates are higher in rural than in urban areas.

The fourth column ("New 3") in Table 3.10 is a further and final modification. Instead of starting from the official rural poverty line for 1993–94 of Rs. 205.67, we start from the corresponding 1987–88 estimate of Rs. 115.7, see again Table 3.7. This is updated to 1993–94 using the All India rural Törnqvist index of 169.8 (Table 3.3.) to give a 1993–94 line of Rs. 196.46. This All India rural poverty line then replaces Rs. 205.67 as the base, and all poverty counts are thereby reduced compared with the previous column. These estimates, like those in the previous column, are the headcount ratios that come out of the price calculations in this paper, and we believe them to be both soundly based and sensible.

The fifth column ("New 43rd") reports the corresponding headcount ratios for the 43rd Round. Again, we start from the All India rural poverty line of 115.7, apply the 43rd Round rural state to All India price indexes (top panel of Table 3.5) to get state level rural poverty lines, which are converted to urban poverty lines using the 43rd Round urban to rural price indexes (top panel of Table 3.4). These headcount ratios are directly comparable to those from the 50th Round in the previous column ("New 3") and the changes in the last column are appropriate measures of the change in poverty between the two rounds. These estimates of change are not very different from those in the final column of Table 3.9, but are to be preferred because of their symmetrical treatment of the two rounds, and because of the fact that they make no use of the implicit urban to rural or statewise price indexes in the official lines. Of course, the levels from which these changes take place are quite different from the official levels, particularly in our much lower poverty rates in urban areas.

Section 5: Further Work and Preliminary Conclusions

The calculations in this paper, although extensive in themselves, leave a great deal undone. In particular, it would be highly desirable to extend the calculations to both earlier periods and later periods. Among the large consumption surveys, the 38th Round (1983) is available and can be used in the same way as the 43rd and the 50th Rounds. The 50th Round is the latest large consumption survey that is currently available, but more recent surveys contain a good deal of consumption information, and could be used to give less precise, but probably still adequate estimates of inflation, if not of interstate or intersectoral price differences. It would also be desirable to extend the indices to cover all of consumption, which could be done by incorporating the appropriate components of the disaggregated CPIAL and CPIIW indexes. The calculations also need to be repeated to check what difference, if any, comes from reweighting our price indexes to more accurately reflect the consumption patterns of the poor. Finally, it would be extremely desirable if the NSS itself were to make similar calculations, as a cross-check, and because independent investigators cannot hope to match the resources, knowledge, and expertise of the government statisticians.

In spite of the preliminary nature of the work, we would like to emphasize some tentative conclusions. First, the unit value data from the NSS consumption surveys are a viable data base for cross-checking other price indexes. Second, the results presented here show good agreement between the rate of increase of the official CPIAL and CPIIW indexes and the prices reported by the large, national sample of respondents in the NSS surveys. Our calculations show little apparent bias in the CPIIW, but suggest that the CPIAL may have been growing too quickly, consistently with what might be expected from using a long outdated Laspeyres rather than a chain-linked or superlative index. If this conclusion is accepted, it is likely that the decline in rural poverty rates has been understated in the official poverty counts. Indeed, we are led to suggest as a working hypothesis that, between 1987–88 and 1993–94, there was no great difference in the rate of decline of urban and rural poverty, at least according to the headcount measure.

Our calculations suggest rather more serious problems with the Expert-Group based current procedures for calculating the official poverty lines. The data examined here suggest that their urban lines are too high relative to their rural lines; we find no support in the NSS purchase data for the argument that urban prices are so much higher than rural prices. Indeed the once standard procedure of assuming a uniform 15 per cent excess of urban over rural prices finds more support in the data than do the current differentials which are around 40 per cent. Nor do the purchase data generate interstate price indexes that are close to those incorporated in the Expert Group and official lines. Although interstate price differences are similar in 1993–94 and 1987–88, they are not identical, and so there is no reason to suppose that interstate price differentials from the early 1960s contain much useful information on price differentials today. There are difficult practical and conceptual problems with the computation of interstate price indexes in a country such as India, and there is a case based on transparency for not trying to do so. But if this case is not accepted, interstate price indexes should be calculated from the plentiful and recent NSS data. Doing so has dramatic effects on the distribution of poverty across the Indian states, and between the rural and urban sectors. Indeed, one of the main results of this paper is that current official practice causes much larger errors in calculating the distribution of poverty within the country than it does in calculating changes in overall poverty over time.

The Expert Group's recommendations are admirable in their attempt to use all the information available in order to improve the updating formulas for the poverty lines. But one unintended consequence of their recommendations has been to make the construction of the lines a great deal less transparent than used to be the case when there were only two lines, one urban and one rural, which were held fixed in real terms, and updated using a single All India price index. Updating now involves two different price indexes, the CPIAL and the CPIIW which are reweighted in a way that makes the poverty lines increase at rates that are (somewhat) different from published price indexes. The base poverty lines that are updated are now also "corrected" for urban to rural price differences, and for interstate differences. As we have seen, these corrections are difficult to make, and any specific numbers are subject to challenge, so that one result has been that there are now several different sets of poverty lines in use by different agencies. Simplicity and transparency are also virtues, and it is legitimate to ask whether the complexity and lack of transparency in the Expert Group's procedures have generated enough additional accuracy to make them worthwhile.

References

Chaterjee, G. S., and N. Bhattacharya, 1974, "Between State Variations in Consumer Prices and Per Capita Household Consumption in Rural India," in T. N. Srinivasan and Pranab Bardhan (eds.), *Poverty and Income Distribution in India*, Calcutta. Statistical Publishing Society.

Deaton, Angus S., 1988, "Quantity, Quality, and Spatial Variation in Price," *American Economic Review*, 78, pp. 418–30.

Deaton, Angus S., 1997, *The Analysis of Household Surveys: A Microeconometric Approach to Development Policy*, Baltimore. Md. Johns Hopkins University Press.

Diewert, W. Erwin, 1976, "Exact and Superlative Index Numbers," *Journal of Econometrics*, 4, pp. 114–45.

Government of India, 1993, *Report of the Expert Group on the Estimation of Proportion and Number of Poor*, Delhi. Planning Commission.

Government of India, 1997, "Estimate of Poverty," Press Information Bureau, March 11th.

Minhas, B.S., L.R. Jain, S.M. Kansal, and M.R. Saluja, 1988, "Measurement of General Cost of Living for Urban India—All India and Different States," *Sarvekshana*, 12.

Pollak, Robert A., 1981, "The Social Cost of Living Index," *Journal of Public Economics*, 15, pp. 311–36.

Prais, Sigbert, 1959, "Whose Cost of Living?" *Review of Economic Studies*, 26, pp. 126–34.

Prais, Sigbert J., and Hendrik S. Houtakker, 1955, *The Analysis of Household Budgets*, Cambridge. Cambridge University Press.

Silverman, Bernard W., 1986, *Density Estimation for Statistics and Data Analysis*, London. Chapman and Hall.

Table 3.1: Numbers of Sample Households and Recorded Purchases

	43rd Round				50th Round			
	Rural		Urban		Rural		Urban	
	Households	Purchases	Households	Purchases	Households	Purchases	Households	Purchases
Andhra Pradesh	6,015	193,490	3,421	122,804	4,908	171,913	3,644	140,384
Assam	3,290	111,468	1,171	40,560	3,199	123,150	880	36,946
Bihar	7,740	194,271	2,083	61,473	6,979	195,356	2,155	71,788
Gujarat	2,795	95,164	2,260	85,016	2,219	85,015	2,372	100,054
Haryana	1,165	37,079	634	22,995	1,040	35,445	697	25,249
Himachal Pradesh	1,835	56,633	459	15,226	1,875	59,905	400	14,664
Jammu & Kashmir	3,197	87,786	1,488	45,082	820	27,606	528	21,050
Karnataka	3,254	120,783	2,307	90,819	2,617	108,986	2,469	106,555
Kerala	3,358	118,107	1,432	49,704	2,555	100,884	1,830	71,601
Madhya Pradesh	6,294	183,849	2,888	104,703	5,313	167,681	3,233	125,399
Maharashtra	5,726	212,872	5,497	222,693	4,440	175,356	5,528	238,136
Orissa	3,493	95,524	1,151	36,628	3,338	105,351	1,037	38,571
Punjab	2,665	84,939	1,901	65,264	2,046	71,961	1,947	72,250
Rajasthan	3,607	89,735	1,734	55,111	3,097	86,723	1,799	60,134
Tamil Nadu	4,567	155,196	4,109	156,221	3,901	155,420	4,042	170,104
Uttar Pradesh	10,395	292,021	4,497	145,020	9,010	297,803	4,451	170,499
West Bengal	4,983	164,005	3,433	124,574	4,480	170,649	3,338	135,564
Delhi	66	2,685	1,130	47,505	61	2,045	985	33,517
All India	82,653	2,531,548	45,348	1,610,434	69,206	2,378,646	46,148	1,807,324

Notes: Households are the numbers of sample households in each round. Purchases are the numbers of recorded purchases of the list of commodities in Table 3.1A.

Table 3.2: Selected Budget Shares and Unit Values, Rural Areas of Two States, 43rd and 50th Rounds

Rural Uttar Pradesh, 50th Round, 1993–94						Rural Kerala, 50th Round, 1993–94					
Commodity	Units	Mean Share	No. of Obs.	Out-liers	Median Unit Value	Commodity	Units	Mean Share	No. of Obs.	Out-liers	Median Unit Value
Atta	kg.	14.3	5,575	39	3.533	Rice: other sources	kg.	10.8	2,073	50	7.5
Milk (liquid)	litre	10.8	6,618	88	6	Rice: P.D.S.	kg.	8.6	1,916	27	5.52
Rice	kg.	9.2	7,186	169	6	Fresh Fish	kg.	5.8	2,158	30	17.6
Mustard Oil	kg.	3.9	8,627	278	30	Milk (liquid)	litre	4.6	1,776	37	8
Firewood & chips	kg.	3.4	4,871	107	0.7	Firewood & chips	kg.	4.6	2,061	49	0.6
Arhar (tur)	kg.	2.6	6,568	210	16	Coconuts	no.	4.5	2,334	25	4
Potatoes	kg.	2.5	8,797	187	3	Coconut oil	kg.	2.8	2,229	50	38
Bidis	no.	1.6	4,802	102	0.071	Tea	cup	2.5	1,698	32	1
Sugar (crystal)	kg.	1.5	5,529	145	12	Sugar: other	kg.	1.6	2,055	13	13.75
Gur (cane)	kg.	1.1	4,770	64	8	Sugar: P.D.S.	kg.	1.1	2,287	48	8.44
Urd	kg.	0.9	4,589	69	12	Bidis	no.	1.5	1,073	20	0.1
Goat meat	kg.	0.9	2,018	16	50	Leaf tea	gm.	1.4	2,248	52	0.065
Leaf tea	gm.	0.7	5,808	113	0.08	Cooked meals	no.	1.3	403	11	7

Rural Uttar Pradesh, 43rd Round, 1987–88						Rural Kerala, 43rd Round, 1987–88					
Commodity	Units	Mean Share	No. of Obs.	Out-liers	Median Unit Value	Commodity	Units	Mean Share	No. of Obs.	Out-liers	Median Unit Value
Atta	kg.	16.5	4,862	26	2	Rice	kg.	20.6	3,271	27	3.6
Milk (liquid)	litre	9.1	7,069	217	4	Coconuts	no.	5.6	3,157	34	3
Rice	kg.	8.9	8,077	130	3.2	Firewood & chips	kg.	5.4	2,984	43	0.43
Mustard oil	kg.	4.7	9,826	96	26	Fresh fish	kg.	5.3	2,777	36	10
Firewood & chips	kg.	3.5	6,845	127	0.5	Milk (liquid)	litre	3.9	2,286	27	4
Arhar (tur)	kg.	3.1	7,305	278	10	Tea	cup	2.7	2,681	34	0.5
Potatoes	kg.	2.3	10,090	59	1.5	Cooked meals	no.	2.5	1,055	33	3.333
Bidis	no.	1.6	5,978	205	0.0333	Sugar	kg.	2.3	3,224	50	5.6
Gur (cane)	kg.	1.5	7,319	235	3.5	Coconut oil	kg.	1.8	2,354	32	34
Sugar (crystal)	kg.	1.3	6,650	37	6.5	Bidis	no.	1.5	1,660	45	0.05
Kerosene	litre	1.1	9,884	156	3	Dried chillies	gm.	1.3	3,255	83	0.02
Urd	kg.	0.9	4,693	169	8	Leaf tea	gm.	1.3	2,857	35	0.0333
Vanaspati	kg.	0.8	2,574	16	26	Palm oil	kg.	1.3	2,034	33	17

Notes: In the 43rd Round foods purchased from the Public Distribution System (P.D.S.) are not distinguished from foods bought from other sources, see for example rice in Kerala in the 43rd Round versus rice in Kerala in the 50th Round. In the 50th round for U.P., the amounts shown for atta, rice, mustard oil, arhar, sugar, and urd are all purchases from sources other than P.D.S. In Kerala for the 50th Round, P.D.S. and other sources both appear in the table except for coconut oil, which is coconut oil from non P.D.S. sources.

Table 3.3: Price Indexes for 1993–94 Relative to 1987–88

	Budget 43	Budget 50	Las-peyres	Paasche Index	Fisher Ideal	Törn-qvist	CPI	PL Deflator
Rural							CPIAL	
Andhra Pradesh	69.9	68.5	177.5	174.1	175.8	175.9	177.3	177.3
Assam	81.9	81.6	174.8	172.5	173.6	173.7	181.6	182.1
Bihar	79.0	76.3	161.3	158.1	159.7	159.7	175.6	176.3
Gujarat	78.5	71.1	175.2	166.1	170.6	170.6	175.2	175.7
Haryana	68.5	69.3	175.7	173.0	174.3	174.2	..	190.2
Himachal Pradesh	68.4	69.2	171.6	162.9	167.1	167.1	..	190.2
Jammu & Kashmir	68.7	67.8	184.9	178.4	181.6	181.5	171.2	..
Karnataka	73.2	62.1	175.8	174.5	175.1	175.1	178.7	178.7
Kerala	69.7	68.5	174.7	169.4	172.1	172.3	186.4	186.7
Madhya Pradesh	75.9	70.9	174.7	169.1	171.9	171.9	179.8	180.5
Maharashtra	71.8	61.1	174.1	171.3	172.7	172.6	168.6	168.6
Orissa	79.9	79.1	167.4	162.1	164.7	164.6	159.9	159.8
Punjab	66.7	68.2	192.6	188.6	190.6	190.7	191.0	190.2
Rajasthan	72.7	68.1	169.4	164.2	166.8	166.9	186.1	183.7
Tamil Nadu	73.4	69.0	169.4	165.9	167.6	167.7	167.0	166.2
Uttar Pradesh	69.8	68.9	170.3	165.5	167.9	167.9	186.0	185.9
West Bengal	79.6	75.5	167.6	165.4	166.5	166.5	170.2	170.8
All India	74.6	70.7	171.7	167.9	169.8	169.8	176.3	178.7
Urban							CPIIW	
Andhra Pradesh	64.8	62.4	179.7	174.6	177.1	177.2	175.9	183.1
Assam	72.4	66.4	179.4	175.9	177.6	177.7	179.7	167.8
Bihar	73.1	71.0	165.9	164.3	165.1	165.2	168.6	158.7
Gujarat	70.4	65.3	169.2	161.7	165.4	165.4	173.0	171.6
Haryana	68.5	60.5	178.6	176.7	177.6	177.6	180.6	180.3
Himachal Pradesh	62.1	58.7	179.7	170.8	175.2	175.2	..	176.0
Jammu & Kashmir	66.8	59.5	185.8	171.7	178.6	178.5	174.3	..
Karnataka	67.7	60.6	179.5	174.6	177.0	177.1	180.8	176.9
Kerala	69.0	63.4	175.5	171.2	173.3	173.5	174.9	171.8
Madhya Pradesh	72.2	63.9	173.5	168.2	170.8	170.9	174.1	177.8
Maharashtra	65.4	59.0	183.4	178.5	180.9	181.1	183.3	173.7
Orissa	70.7	66.6	169.1	166.5	167.8	167.8	178.7	180.3
Punjab	62.5	60.9	188.6	185.4	187.0	187.1	172.4	174.9
Rajasthan	67.1	64.5	173.7	169.9	171.8	171.8	173.1	169.8
Tamil Nadu	62.9	62.9	172.4	168.3	170.3	170.5	177.1	178.9
Uttar Pradesh	67.2	64.7	166.5	164.2	165.4	165.4	169.6	167.8
West Bengal	68.4	65.3	172.4	168.8	170.6	170.6	172.1	165.1
Delhi	55.8	56.9	180.1	170.5	175.2	175.7	177.1	174.9
All India	67.6	63.4	175.1	172.3	173.7	173.8	175.1	173.5

Notes: Budget 43 and Budget 50 are the total shares of the budget (in per cent) in the 43rd and 50th Rounds respectively of all the goods covered by the index. Data for All India are calculated from the complete survey, including those states and territories not listed separately. We do not have data for the CPIAL for Haryana nor for Jammu & Kashmir, nor the CPIIW for Jammu & Kashmir. The final column is the implicit deflator of the official poverty lines; it is computed from the same prices collected for the CPIAL and CPIIW, but uses different weights in order to more closely reflect the experience of people near the poverty line.

Table 3.4: Price Indexes for Urban Relative to Rural, 43rd and 50th Rounds

	Budget: Urban	Budget: Rural	Laspeyres Index	Paasche Index	Fisher Ideal Index	Törnqvist Index	PL Deflator	Uncovered Price
43rd Round								
Andhra Pradesh	68.8	74.7	111.8	109.5	110.6	110.7	165.2	456.6
Assam	75.0	83.5	109.1	107.0	108.1	108.0	99.3	72.1
Bihar	75.5	80.4	108.5	107.7	108.1	108.1	124.8	207.6
Gujarat	72.7	80.0	106.3	104.5	105.4	105.4	150.6	476.5
Haryana	71.5	69.4	114.1	110.3	112.2	112.1	116.5	127.8
Himachal Pradesh	66.5	67.8	111.6	96.1	103.6	104.8	117.2	147.5
Jammu & Kashmir	72.5	72.5	104.6	102.8	103.7	103.8	119.3	172.4
Karnataka	71.4	77.2	110.4	108.9	109.6	110.0	163.9	518.8
Kerala	73.0	74.4	103.7	103.4	103.5	103.5	125.0	212.3
Madhya Pradesh	74.2	76.6	116.9	109.4	113.1	113.0	166.7	548.7
Maharashtra	69.1	73.8	114.9	113.1	114.0	114.1	163.6	403.4
Orissa	73.5	81.2	112.9	107.6	110.2	110.2	136.2	281.0
Punjab	64.7	68.6	115.6	110.8	113.2	113.2	118.0	128.1
Rajasthan	70.2	74.3	108.2	105.3	106.7	106.7	140.7	289.3
Tamil Nadu	68.8	79.3	109.7	108.4	109.0	109.0	140.3	288.0
Uttar Pradesh	69.7	71.8	120.0	116.1	118.1	118.1	134.6	184.4
West Bengal	71.9	81.8	112.9	112.4	112.6	112.7	116.1	127.9
All India	70.9	77.1	113.1	109.8	111.4	111.4	140.8	274.0
50th Round								
Andhra Pradesh	63.4	69.6	111.8	109.3	110.5	110.5	170.6	404.1
Assam	68.3	80.9	113.6	109.1	111.3	111.6	91.5	51.2
Bihar	71.7	77.0	112.6	112.3	112.5	112.5	112.4	112.2
Gujarat	67.6	74.6	106.9	103.4	105.1	105.2	147.1	335.3
Haryana	62.3	69.1	119.2	112.0	115.5	115.6	110.5	101.2
Himachal Pradesh	61.4	66.8	110.9	104.5	107.7	108.1	108.5	109.2
Jammu & Kashmir	58.2	67.1	109.2	104.9	107.0	107.0	n.a.	n.a.
Karnataka	64.3	69.1	111.3	109.9	110.6	110.6	162.3	349.9
Kerala	64.0	68.6	104.7	103.7	104.2	104.2	115.1	139.8
Madhya Pradesh	65.1	73.3	118.7	113.1	115.8	115.8	164.2	360.1
Maharashtra	61.7	67.4	121.2	115.4	118.3	118.2	168.5	321.6
Orissa	66.4	77.9	111.9	108.9	110.4	110.5	153.7	361.3
Punjab	62.8	68.5	116.3	112.0	114.1	114.2	108.5	98.3
Rajasthan	64.9	72.6	113.2	109.1	111.1	111.3	130.1	183.4
Tamil Nadu	63.3	70.1	111.0	108.5	109.8	109.7	150.9	286.0
Uttar Pradesh	66.2	69.2	118.3	114.5	116.4	116.5	121.4	132.4
West Bengal	65.3	75.4	119.6	115.0	117.3	117.5	112.1	100.4
All India	65.8	73.7	117.5	113.7	115.6	115.6	136.7	201.1

Table 3.5: Price Indexes for States Relative to All India, 43rd Round, 1987-88

	Share of Budget	Laspeyres Index	Paasche Index	Fisher Ideal Index	Törnqvist Index Implicit	Poverty Lines
Rural						
Andhra Pradesh	75.5	98.3	90.9	94.6	94.0	79.8
Assam	84.3	108.1	104.2	106.1	106.7	110.6
Bihar	81.2	104.4	104.5	104.5	104.6	104.5
Gujarat	80.4	111.3	110.0	110.5	110.5	99.8
Haryana	70.4	104.0	94.7	99.3	98.9	106.7
Himachal Pradesh	70.8	103.9	100.0	101.9	101.6	106.7
Jammu & Kashmir	73.7	97.9	92.9	95.4	95.1	107.9
Karnataka	77.6	102.6	97.1	99.8	99.3	90.7
Kerala	74.7	111.5	99.2	105.2	104.9	113.4
Madhya Pradesh	77.8	96.6	92.9	94.8	94.2	92.9
Maharashtra	74.5	105.2	102.7	103.9	103.8	100.4
Orissa	82.4	99.1	94.3	96.7	96.6	105.4
Punjab	68.8	100.2	88.8	94.3	94.2	106.7
Rajasthan	75.3	112.2	97.7	104.7	103.9	102.0
Tamil Nadu	79.6	109.4	102.9	106.1	105.5	102.6
Uttar Pradesh	72.0	94.6	88.2	91.3	91.4	99.5
West Bengal	82.1	100.2	98.3	99.2	99.2	112.2
All India	71.0*	100.0	100.0	100.0	100.0	100.0
Urban						
Andhra Pradesh	69.0	96.8	91.4	94.1	94.0	93.6
Assam	75.0	104.4	101.0	102.7	103.0	78.1
Bihar	75.7	102.6	98.7	100.6	100.5	92.7
Gujarat	73.3	112.0	107.9	110.0	109.5	106.8
Haryana	71.7	102.8	100.3	101.6	101.5	88.3
Himachal Pradesh	66.7	101.0	94.9	97.9	98.2	88.8
Jammu & Kashmir	72.6	94.9	90.3	92.6	92.2	91.5
Karnataka	71.6	99.6	96.8	98.2	98.2	105.6
Kerala	73.1	103.0	92.4	97.5	97.6	100.7
Madhya Pradesh	75.6	100.4	96.6	98.5	98.2	110.0
Maharashtra	69.4	109.1	106.6	107.9	107.8	116.7
Orissa	74.0	96.3	91.5	93.8	94.0	102.0
Punjab	64.9	99.3	94.7	97.0	96.6	89.4
Rajasthan	70.5	106.8	97.5	102.1	101.5	102.0
Tamil Nadu	68.9	102.0	99.8	100.9	100.8	102.2
Uttar Pradesh	69.8	102.0	96.3	99.1	98.8	95.1
West Bengal	72.2	102.8	98.4	100.6	100.1	92.5
Delhi	60.2	105.1	102.2	103.7	102.8	109.1
All India	66.5*	100.0	100.0	100.0	100.0	100.0

Note: *Indicates the average over all the states. The implicit Expert Group price index is obtained from Table 3.1 of the Expert Group report by dividing the state poverty lines by the All India poverty lines.

Table 3.6: Price Indexes for States Relative to All India, 50th Round, 1994–95

	Share of budget	Laspeyres Index	Paasche Index	Fisher Ideal Index	Törnqvist Index Implicit	Poverty Lines
Rural						
Andhra Pradesh	71.1	104.8	93.5	99.0	97.9	79.2
Assam	81.9	114.4	104.6	109.4	109.3	112.7
Bihar	77.4	98.9	96.9	97.9	98.1	103.1
Gujarat	75.4	118.7	114.5	116.6	116.5	98.2
Haryana	69.7	107.2	99.8	103.4	103.3	113.6
Himachal Pradesh	74.2	107.4	101.6	104.5	104.5	113.6
Jammu & Kashmir	71.1	105.9	102.2	104.0	104.1	..
Karnataka	72.8	105.7	101.7	103.7	103.5	90.7
Kerala	68.7	119.5	105.7	112.4	112.7	118.5
Madhya Pradesh	74.2	95.6	93.0	94.3	94.2	93.8
Maharashtra	69.5	110.0	100.7	105.2	105.7	94.7
Orissa	80.0	99.0	87.4	93.0	92.8	94.3
Punjab	68.9	109.9	101.1	105.4	105.0	113.6
Rajasthan	73.3	112.2	100.7	106.3	105.5	104.9
Tamil Nadu	70.8	114.1	102.0	107.9	107.0	95.5
Uttar Pradesh	70.0	94.8	89.4	92.1	91.8	103.5
West Bengal	75.6	99.7	94.2	96.9	96.6	107.2
All India	66.9*	100.0	100.0	100.0	100.0	100.0
Urban						
Andhra Pradesh	63.6	98.0	90.9	94.4	94.0	98.9
Assam	68.6	109.1	102.4	105.7	105.9	75.5
Bihar	72.0	98.1	93.4	95.8	95.7	84.8
Gujarat	68.2	105.8	104.6	105.2	105.2	105.6
Haryana	63.0	101.6	100.1	100.9	100.9	91.8
Himachal Pradesh	61.7	101.4	97.3	99.4	99.3	90.1
Jammu & Kashmir	62.3	97.3	94.3	95.8	95.7	..
Karnataka	64.4	101.4	98.0	99.7	99.4	107.7
Kerala	64.1	106.8	94.9	100.7	100.5	99.7
Madhya Pradesh	65.6	95.6	94.0	94.8	94.8	112.7
Maharashtra	62.2	112.2	108.9	110.6	110.6	116.8
Orissa	67.7	93.8	87.1	90.4	90.6	106.0
Punjab	63.2	103.2	100.4	101.8	101.7	90.1
Rajasthan	65.6	104.9	95.8	100.2	99.7	99.8
Tamil Nadu	63.5	105.1	97.1	101.0	100.4	105.4
Uttar Pradesh	66.3	96.8	91.9	94.3	94.1	91.9
West Bengal	65.6	103.2	97.5	100.3	100.0	88.0
Delhi	58.6	109.3	103.4	106.3	106.3	110.0
All India	60.5*	100.0	100.0	100.0	100.0	100.0

Note: *Indicates the average over all states.

Table 3.7: Official Poverty Lines and Headcount Ratios, 43rd and 50th Round

	Poverty Lines 1987–88	Headcount Ratio 1987–88	Poverty Lines 1993–94	Headcount Ratio 1993–94	Change in HCR
Rural					
Andhra Pradesh	91.94	21.04	163.02	15.89	–5.15
Assam	127.44	39.42	232.05	45.20	5.78
Bihar	120.36	53.92	212.16	57.95	4.03
Gujarat	115.00	28.56	202.11	22.16	–6.40
Haryana	122.90	15.34	233.79	28.26	12.92
Himachal Pradesh	122.90	16.68	233.79	30.36	13.68
Karnataka	104.46	32.63	186.63	30.11	–2.52
Kerala	130.61	29.46	243.84	25.38	–4.08
Madhya Pradesh	107.00	42.02	193.10	40.72	–1.30
Maharashtra	115.61	40.95	194.94	37.91	–3.04
Orissa	121.42	58.67	194.03	49.84	–8.83
Punjab	122.90	12.81	233.79	11.69	–1.12
Rajasthan	117.52	33.30	215.89	26.40	–6.90
Tamil Nadu	118.23	46.34	196.53	32.95	–13.39
Uttar Pradesh	114.57	41.92	213.01	42.32	0.40
West Bengal	129.21	48.80	220.74	41.18	–7.62
All India (1)	115.20	39.01	205.84	37.21	–1.80
All India (2)	115.70	39.40	205.67	37.13	–2.42
Urban					
Andhra Pradesh	151.88	41.09	278.14	38.82	–2.27
Assam	126.60	11.32	212.42	7.93	–3.39
Bihar	150.25	51.89	238.49	34.84	–17.05
Gujarat	173.18	38.53	297.22	28.26	–10.27
Haryana	143.22	18.38	258.23	16.47	–1.91
Himachal Pradesh	144.10	7.20	253.61	9.26	2.06
Karnataka	171.18	49.19	302.89	39.90	–9.29
Kerala	163.29	39.80	280.54	24.31	–15.49
Madhya Pradesh	178.35	47.25	317.16	48.08	0.83
Maharashtra	189.17	40.34	328.56	34.99	–5.35
Orissa	165.40	42.58	298.22	40.64	–1.94
Punjab	144.98	13.70	253.61	10.90	–2.80
Rajasthan	165.38	37.89	280.85	31.02	–6.87
Tamil Nadu	165.82	40.20	296.63	39.91	–0.29
Uttar Pradesh	154.15	44.93	258.65	35.09	–9.84
West Bengal	149.96	33.74	247.53	22.95	–10.79
Delhi	176.91	15.06	309.48	16.09	1.03
All India (1)	162.16	38.64	281.35	32.63	–6.01
All India (2)	163.30	39.10	283.44	33.15	–5.80

Notes: The first and third columns, the two sets of poverty lines by state and sector, are those used by the Planning Commission in the official poverty counts. The headcount ratios in the second and fourth columns are computed from the unit record data from the 43rd and 50th Rounds, and estimate the proportions of people below the poverty line for the state and sector in which they live. These differ slightly from the official headcount ratios because the official calculations use grouped data; the numbers in the Table are therefore somewhat more accurate than the official estimates. The All India (1) headcount ratios are computed from the official All India rural and urban poverty lines as shown.; Rupees 115.20 (rural) and 162.16 (urban) in the 43rd Round, and 205.84 (rural) and 281.35 (urban) in the 50th Round. The All India headcount ratios are the fractions of people in rural and urban India whose household per capita expenditure is below these lines. However, in the official methodology, these All India lines are calculated implicitly from the state level results; the headcount ratios for each state and territory are added up (weighted by population) to give an All India headcount ratio, and an All India poverty line calculated so as to yield that headcount ratio when directly applied to the All India data. These calculations are replicated in the row labeled All India. (2) We have followed the official methodology in assigning poverty lines or poverty rates to small states as follows: Goa and Dadra & Nagar Haveli are assigned the poverty lines of Maharashtra, and rural Delhi (not shown in the Table) the poverty line of rural Haryana. Other small states and territories are assigned the poverty rates of neighbors with rural matched to rural and urban to urban: Assam is used for Arunachal Pradesh, Manipur, Meghalaya, Mizoram, Nagaland, Sikkim, and Tripura; Tamil Nadu is used for the Andaman & Nicobar Islands and for Pondicherry; the urban poverty rate for Punjab is assigned to both rural and urban households in Chandigarh; Maharashtra is used for Daman & Diu; and Kerala for Lakshadweep. In the 50th Round, the headcount ratio for Himachal Pradesh is used for Jammu & Kashmir. Assigning neighboring poverty rates appears to be a less attractive strategy than assigning neighboring poverty lines; the assumption that the price levels are the same is surely more appropriate than the assumption that the lower tails of the consumption distribution are similar. However, the small states and territories contain a small enough share of the population so that differences in methodology do not have much effect. Using poverty lines rather than poverty rates, the All India rural lines and headcount ratios are 115.50 rupees and 39.24 per cent in the 43rd Round and 204.95 rupees and 36.84 per cent in the 50th Round. The corresponding urban estimates are 163.24 rupees and 39.08 per cent in the 43rd Round and 282.11 rupees and 32.83 per cent in the 50th Round.

Table 3.8: Official Price Indexes and Implicit Price Deflators: 1993–94 versus 1987–88

	CPIAL	Implicit Rural Price Deflator	CPIIW	Implicit Urban Price Deflator
Andhra Pradesh	177.3	177.3	175.9	183.1
Assam	181.6	182.1	179.7	167.8
Bihar	175.6	176.3	168.6	158.7
Gujarat	175.2	175.7	173.0	171.6
Haryana	..	190.2	180.6	180.3
Karnataka	178.7	178.7	180.8	176.9
Kerala	186.4	186.7	174.9	171.8
Madhya Pradesh	179.8	180.5	174.1	177.8
Maharashtra	168.6	168.6	183.3	173.7
Orissa	159.9	159.8	178.7	180.3
Punjab	191.0	190.2	172.4	174.9
Rajasthan	186.1	183.7	173.1	169.8
Tamil Nadu	167.0	166.2	177.1	178.9
Uttar Pradesh	186.0	185.9	169.6	167.8
West Bengal	170.2	170.8	172.1	165.1
All India	176.3	178.7	175.1	173.5

Notes: The CPIAL and CPIIW are repeated from Table 3.3. The implicit rural and urban price deflators come from the Planning Commission's poverty lines are obtained by dividing the 1993–94 poverty lines by the 1987–88 lines.

Table 3.9: Sensitivity of Headcount Ratios and Alternative Estimates

	ΔHCR 43	ΔHCR 50	ΔlnP	HCR50	HCR50 New	Change 43–50	Change 43–50 New
Rural							
Andhra Pradesh	0.70	0.56	−0.8	15.89	15.49	−5.15	−5.55
Assam	1.11	1.17	−4.7	45.20	39.51	5.78	0.09
Bihar	1.11	0.87	−9.9	57.95	48.37	4.03	−5.55
Gujarat	0.93	0.76	−3.0	22.16	20.26	−6.40	−8.30
Haryana	0.70	0.73	−8.8	28.26	20.49	12.91	5.15
Himachal Pradesh	0.74	0.91	−13.0	30.36	17.14	13.68	0.46
Karnataka	0.84	1.00	−2.0	30.11	28.07	−2.52	−4.56
Kerala	0.92	0.66	−8.0	25.38	20.49	−4.08	−8.97
Madhya Pradesh	0.97	0.91	−4.9	40.72	36.16	−1.30	−5.86
Maharashtra	0.85	0.74	2.3	37.91	39.65	−3.04	−1.30
Orissa	0.93	1.03	3.0	49.84	52.68	−8.83	−5.99
Punjab	0.62	0.64	0.2	11.69	11.98	−1.12	−0.83
Rajasthan	0.80	0.92	−9.6	26.40	18.66	−6.90	−14.64
Tamil Nadu	0.78	0.86	0.9	32.95	33.41	−13.39	−12.93
Uttar Pradesh	0.88	0.86	−10.2	42.32	33.76	0.40	−8.16
West Bengal	0.89	0.96	−2.6	41.18	38.71	−7.62	−10.09
All India	0.89	0.91	−5.1	37.21	32.78	−1.80	−6.23
Urban							
Andhra Pradesh	0.74	0.77	−3.3	38.82	35.83	−2.27	−5.26
Assam	0.46	0.66	5.7	7.93	10.82	−3.39	−0.50
Bihar	0.88	0.91	4.0	34.84	38.32	−17.05	−13.57
Gujarat	0.96	0.62	−3.7	28.28	26.10	−10.27	−12.43
Haryana	0.70	0.46	−1.5	16.47	15.79	−1.91	−2.59
Himachal Pradesh	0.32	0.32	−0.5	9.26	9.26	2.06	2.06
Karnataka	0.80	0.66	0.1	39.90	40.11	−9.29	−9.08
Kerala	0.78	0.69	1.0	24.31	25.16	−15.49	−14.64
Madhya Pradesh	0.77	0.69	−4.0	48.08	45.08	0.83	−2.17
Maharashtra	0.57	0.66	4.2	34.99	38.08	−5.35	−2.26
Orissa	0.98	0.80	−7.2	40.64	35.67	−1.94	−6.91
Punjab	0.57	0.66	6.7	10.90	14.43	−2.80	0.74
Rajasthan	0.75	0.77	1.2	31.02	31.93	−6.87	−5.96
Tamil Nadu	0.73	0.84	4.8	39.91	35.87	−0.29	−4.33
Uttar Pradesh	0.81	0.82	−1.4	35.09	33.76	−9.84	−11.17
West Bengal	0.91	0.56	3.3	22.95	24.57	−10.79	−9.17
Delhi	0.57	0.57	0.4	16.09	16.50	1.03	1.44
All India	0.69	0.73	0.2	32.62	32.78	−6.01	−5.87

Notes: ΔHCR is the estimated derivative of the headcount ratio with respect to the logarithm of the updating price index; it is also the derivative with respect to the logarithm of mean pce with the distribution held constant. ΔlnP is the logarithm of our Törnqvist price index less the logarithm of the official price index implicit in the poverty lines, and is the difference between the logarithms of column 8 and column 6 in Table 3.3. HCR50 is replicated from Table 3.7. HCR50 new is the headcount ratio in 1993–94 when, instead of the official lines for the 50th Round, we use the official lines for the 43rd Round updated using the Törnqvist indexes in Table 3.3. The change for 43–50 is replicated from Table 3.7, and the new change 43–50 is the difference between the HCR43 (Table 3.7) and HCR50 new.

Table 3.10: Official and Alternative Headcount Ratios for 1993–94 and Change Since 1987–88

	Official	New 1	New 2	New 3	New 43rd	Change
Rural						
Andhra Pradesh	15.89	15.89	33.47	29.17	35.00	–5.83
Assam	45.20	45.20	41.51	35.43	36.13	–0.70
Bihar	57.95	57.95	53.21	48.57	54.55	–5.98
Gujarat	22.16	22.16	37.22	32.45	39.43	–6.98
Haryana	28.26	28.26	19.67	17.01	13.58	3.43
Himachal Pradesh	30.36	30.36	21.15	17.14	13.26	3.88
Jammu & Kashmir	n.a.	n.a.	13.66	10.13	15.32	–5.19
Karnataka	30.11	30.11	42.46	37.90	40.81	–2.91
Kerala	25.38	25.38	22.36	19.48	23.77	–4.29
Madhya Pradesh	40.72	40.72	41.11	36.63	43.72	–7.09
Maharashtra	37.91	37.91	46.69	42.89	44.32	–1.43
Orissa	49.84	49.84	47.78	43.50	50.37	–6.87
Punjab	11.69	11.69	8.56	6.16	6.61	–0.45
Rajasthan	26.40	26.40	26.79	23.03	35.29	–12.26
Tamil Nadu	32.95	32.95	43.18	38.46	49.01	–10.55
Uttar Pradesh	42.32	42.32	32.35	28.65	34.92	–6.27
West Bengal	41.18	41.18	29.23	25.07	36.29	–11.22
All India	37.13	37.13	37.10	32.94	38.96	–6.02
Urban						
Andhra Pradesh	38.82	9.61	20.75	17.78	23.44	–5.66
Assam	7.93	17.93	16.26	12.97	13.56	–0.59
Bihar	34.84	34.97	30.47	26.68	38.13	–11.45
Gujarat	28.28	8.08	17.62	14.72	16.42	–1.70
Haryana	16.46	18.99	14.85	10.55	11.79	–1.24
Himachal Pradesh	9.26	9.26	5.61	3.64	1.66	1.98
Jammu & Kashmir	n.a.	n.a.	3.89	3.10	3.82	–0.72
Karnataka	39.90	16.03	24.50	21.44	25.95	–4.51
Kerala	24.31	18.34	15.98	13.87	20.97	–7.10
Madhya Pradesh	48.08	20.83	21.22	18.50	20.70	–2.20
Maharashtra	34.99	15.67	20.57	18.24	21.16	–2.92
Orissa	40.64	18.97	17.89	15.18	20.82	–5.64
Punjab	10.90	14.19	9.11	7.75	6.56	1.19
Rajasthan	31.02	20.37	20.75	18.26	19.80	–1.54
Tamil Nadu	39.91	16.13	24.20	20.85	26.15	–5.30
Uttar Pradesh	35.09	32.13	24.15	21.71	29.29	–7.58
West Bengal	22.95	25.19	18.99	15.53	22.26	–6.73
All India, weighted average	33.15	19.33	20.83	18.12	22.83	–4.71

Notes: The first column, "Official" repeats the Planning Commission's poverty counts for 1993–94, and thus repeats column 4 of Table 3.7. In the second column, labeled "New 1," we take the Planning Commission's rural poverty lines as given, so that the rural figures are the same as in the first column. However, the urban poverty lines are calculated using the Planning Commission's rural poverty lines and multiplying by the urban to rural Törnqvist price indexes reported in the bottom panel of Table 3.4. The third column, labeled "New 2" uses only the All India rural poverty line (205.67, see Table 3.7) from our reworking of the official counts. The rural lines for each state are created from the All India line using the state Törnqvist price indexes from the top panel of Table 3.6, and the urban lines are created from the rural lines using the urban to rural price indexes as in column 2. Note that the All India rural poverty rate in column 3, 37.10 per cent, is not identical to the figure of 37.13 reported in column 1 and in Table 3.7; this small discrepancy comes from the treatment of the All India headcount ratio, which is derived here by imputing poverty lines or poverty rates to the small states (see the notes to Table 3.7 for details) and in addition using the official lines for urban and rural Delhi, and then weighting the state poverty rates by their shares in the population. Presumably, the discrepancy could be eliminated by some iterative calculation. Column 4, labeled "New 3," uses the All India official poverty line (as recalculated here) for 1987–88, 115.70, see Table 3.7. This is updated to 1993–94 using the All India Törnqvist rural price index, 169.8 from Table 3.3. The rural and urban state level poverty lines are then created as in column 3. Column 5, labeled "New 43rd" uses the corresponding procedure for the 43rd Round, starting from 115.70, and creating rural poverty lines from the state indexes from the 43rd Round, and converting to urban lines using the urban to rural price indexes for the 43rd Round. The final column, labeled "Change" is the column 5 minus column 4 and shows the estimated change in the headcount ratios using the preferred methodology. In all cases, the All India headcount ratios are derived from the state ratios following the "official" methodology, imputing lines or rates to the small states, and adding over all states with the appropriate population weights, see notes to Table 3.7. In these calculations, the official lines for Delhi are used when needed; this avoids the need to calculate a rural price index from the small sample of households in rural Delhi.

Table 3.1A: List of Commodities in 50th Round

Paddy	Urd - P.D.S.	Eggs	Mango	Cooked Meals
Rice - P.D.S.	Urd - other sources	Egg Products	Kharbooza	Cake, Pastry
Rice - other sources	Khesari - P.D.S.	Fish (fresh)	Pears (naspati)	Pickles
Chira	Khesari - other	Fish (dry)	Berries	Sauce
Khoi, Lawa	Peas	Fish (canned)	Leechi	Jam/Jelly
Muri	Soyabean	Other meat, etc.	Apple	Other Proc Food
Other Rice Products	Other Pulses	Potato	Grapes	Pan, leaf
Wheat - P.D.S.	Besan	Onion	Other Fresh Fruits	Pan, finished
Wheat - other	Other Pulse Products	Radish	Coconut (copra)	Supari
Atta - P.D.S.	Milk, Liquid	Carrot	Groundnut	Lime
Atta - other sources	Baby Food	Turnip	Dates	Katha
Maida	Milk, cond./Powder	Beet	Cashew Nuts	Other Pan Ingredients
Suji, Rawa	Curd	Sweet Potato	Walnuts	Bidi
Seewai, Noodles	Ghee	Arum	Other Nuts	Cigarettes
Bread, Bakery	Butter	Other Root Veg.	Raisins (kishmish)	Leaf Tobacco
Other Wheat Products	Ice-cream	Pumpkin	Other Dry Fruits	Snuff
Jowar - P.D.S.	Other Milk Products	Gourd	Sugar (crystal) PDS	Hookah Tobacco
Jowar - other	Vanaspati - P.D.S.	Bitter Gourd	Sugar (crystal) other	Cheroot
Jowar Products	Vanaspati - other	Cucumber	Khandsari	Zarda, Kimam, Serti
Bajra - P.D.S.	Margarine	Parwal/Patal	Gur (cane)	Other Tobacco Products
Bajra - other	Mustard Oil - P.D.S.	Jhinga/Torai	Gur (others)	Ganja
Bajra Products	Mustard Oil - other	Snake Gourd	Sugar Candy (misri)	Toddy

Contd...

Maize - P.D.S.	Groundnut Oil, P.D.S.	Other Gourd	Honey	Country Liquor
Maize - other	Groundnut Oil -other	Cauliflower	Sugar (others)	Opium, Bhangharas
Maize Products	Coconut Oil - P.D.S.	Cabbage	Sea Salt	Beer
Barley	Coconut Oil - other	Brinjal	Other Salt	Foreign Ref.Liquor
Barley Products	Gingelly Oil - P.D.S.	Lady's Finger	Turmeric	Other Drugs and
Small Millets	Gingelly Oil - other	Palak	Black Pepper	Intoxicants
Small Millets products	Linseed Oil - P.D.S.	Other Leafy Veg.	Dry Chillies	Coke
Ragi	Linseed Oil - other	French Beans	Garlic	Firewood and Chips
Ragi Products	Refined Oil - P.D.S.	Tomato	Tamarind	Electricity
Gram (whole grain)	Refined Oil - other	Peas	Ginger	Dung Cake
Gram Products	Palm Oil - P.D.S.	Chili (green)	Curry Powder	Kerosene - P.D.S.
Tapioca/Sago	Palm Oil - other	Capsicum	Other Spices	Kerosene - other
Tapioca (green)	Rapeseed Oil P.D.S.	Plantain (green)	Tea, cups	Matches
Mahua	Rapeseed Oil - other	Jackfruit (green)	Tea, leaf	Coal - P.D.S.
Jackfruit seed	Oil seeds	Lemon	Coffee, cups	Coal - other sources
Other Cereal Subs	Edible Oils (others)	Other Vegetables	Coffee, powder	Coal Gas
Arhar (tur) - P.D.S.	Goat Meat	Banana	Ice	L.P.G.
Arhar - other	Mutton	Jackfruit	Cold Beverage	Charcoal
Gram (split) - P.D.S.	Beef	Water Melon	Fruit Juice, Shake	Other Lighting Oils
Gram (split) - other	Pork	Pineapple	Coconut, green	Candles
Moong - P.D.S.	Buffalo Meat	Coconut	Other Beverages	Methylated Spirits
Moong - other	Other Meat	Guava	Biscuits & Confect	Gobar Gas
Masur - P.D.S.	Chicken	Singara	Salted Refreshment	Other Fuel and
Masur - other	Other Birds	Orange, Mausami	Prepared Sweets	Light

Table 3.2A: List of Commodities Excluded Because of Lack of Quantity Data

Egg products	Salted refreshments	Dung cakes
Other fresh fruit	Prepared sweets	Gobar gas
Other beverages	Other processed food	Other fuel and light
Biscuits & confectionery	Other drugs and intoxicants	

Table 3.3A: List of Commodities Excluded from 43rd Round Calculations (in addition to those listed in Table 3.2A)

Other wheat products	Other dried fruit	Other oil for lighting
Ice cream	Ice	LPG
Other milk products	Fruit juice/shakes	Candles
Other nuts	Other pan ingredients	Methylated spirits

Table 3.4A: List of Commodities Excluded from 50th Round Calculations (in addition to those listed in Table 3.2A)

Other cereal substitutes	Coconuts	Other pan ingredients
Other spices	Tea (cups)	Hookah tobacco
Ice cream	Coffee powder	Opium
Other milk products	Ice	Toddy
Other birds	Cold drinks	Other oil for lighting
Other meat, eggs, and fish	Cakes and pastries	
Other nuts	Pan leaf	

Table 3.5A: List of Commodities Excluded from 43rd and 50th Round Comparisons (in addition to the union of commodities listed in Tables 3.4A and 3.5A)

Goods whose units changed	Goods whose units appear to have changed
Lemons	Coal gas
Guavas	Cheroots
	Zarda, kimam and serti
	Other tobacco
	Ganja

Urban Poverty Reduction Strategies: Past, Present and Future*

4

Tara Ramanathan and *Paramita Datta Dey*

I. URBAN POVERTY: AN INCONVENIENT TRUTH

Global Status of Urban Poverty

The immense inequality gap between the 'haves' and the 'have nots' is and has always been a reality around the world. Poverty is the state for a majority of the world's people and nations. In developing countries, where more than 1 person in 5 subsists on less than $1 a day, poverty kills, and in extreme cases people end their own lives to escape from poverty. "Half the world — nearly 3 billion people — lives on less than $2 a day. 1 billion children live in poverty (1 in 2 children in the world). About 640 million people live without adequate shelter, 400 million have no access to safe water, and 270 million have no access to health services. "Less than 1% of what the world spent every year on weapon's was needed to put every child into school by the year 2000 and yet it didn't happen[1]." These are, without a doubt, some of the major causes of poverty in the world. However, there are deeper and more global causes of poverty that are not adequately discussed.

Poverty: A Global Priority?

Though we have all been aware of the widespread existence of poverty for a while, it still continues to persist in spite of all the efforts dedicated towards alleviating poverty. One of the root causes of this seemingly permanent inequality is the lack of a global concern for the poor. Since the existence of poverty

* *Courtesy*: www.niua.org

does not directly affect a majority of us, we do not put much effort towards rescuing the poor. However, since poverty is a multi-dimensional problem, it requires the aid of more stakeholders than just NGOs or CBOs. In order to effectively and efficiently alleviate poverty, global stakeholders, including local and state governments, must keep poverty reduction as one of their top priorities. So far governments have not put forth the significant amount of effort necessary to create solidarity between their work, the work of NGOs and any other stakeholders putting forth Urban Poverty Reduction Strategies (UPRS). Thus, it will remain global trend for the gap between the rich and poor to rapidly widen until poverty reduction becomes a global priority.

Table 4.1[1]: Examples of Global Priorities in Spending in 1998

Global Priority	*$U.S. Billions*
Cosmetics in the United States	8
Ice cream in Europe	11
Perfumes in Europe and the United States	12
Pet foods in Europe and the United States	17
Business entertainment in Japan	35
Cigarettes in Europe	50
Alcoholic drinks in Europe	105
Narcotics drugs in the world	400
Military spending in the world	780

And compare that to what was estimated as 'additional' costs to achieve universal access to basic social services in all developing countries:

Global Priority	*$U.S. Billions*
Basic education for all	6
Water and sanitation for all	9
Reproductive health for all women	12
Basic health and nutrition	13

Global Poverty Status: Making Progress

Due to a fortunate shift of attention from perfume to poverty, global living standards have risen dramatically over the last decades. "The proportion of the developing world's population living in extreme economic poverty — defined as living on less than $1 per day ($1.08 in 1993, adjusted to account for differences in purchasing power across countries) — has fallen from 28% in 1990 to 21% in 2001. Poverty also fell in South Asia over the past 20 years, and while the decline was not as rapid, almost 45 million fewer people were living in extreme poverty by 2001."[2]

Problem solved?

While there has been great progress in reducing poverty, the global picture masks large regional differences. Global trends in poverty reduction have been dominated by rapid growth in China and the East Asia and Pacific region. The performance in three other regions: Africa, Latin America, and South Asia; shows only moderate or no declines in the incidence of poverty, while the number of people in poverty in these regions has increased. "In Sub-Saharan Africa, an additional 74 million people joined the ranks of the poor reaching a total of 291 million in 1998. In Latin America the figure increased from 64 to 78 million and in South Asia a total of 522 million people live in poverty. Countries in Eastern Europe and Central Asia experienced an increase in both the incidence of poverty and the number of people living below the international poverty line. Here, the incidence rose from 2% to 5%, translating into 24 million people more in poverty."[3]

Urban Poverty not being Addressed

In addition, the before mentioned decrease in poverty rate ignores the detrimental impact that urbanization has had and will have on the poverty rate. In 2007, for the first time in history, the world's urban population was expected exceed the rural population. The biggest cities are growing faster than smaller towns[4]. India's mega-cities have the highest percentage of slum-dwellers in the country. This indicates that as big cities grow even larger, their slums will swell. By 2030 there will be

5 billion people living in cities. Cities of the developing world will make up 95% of urban expansion in the next two decades and by 2030, cities will be home to 80% of the world's urban population (4 billion people). "Over half of the world's urban population will be living in Asia (2.66 billion). More Africans will be living in cities than the total population of Europe (748 million). The fastest urban growth, spurred by migration from the countryside, will occur in small cities and towns of less than 1 million inhabitants."[4]

Urbanization: A Positive Change?

While urban growth can be seen as positive for the economy, it is actually a serious problem. As cities grow, their slum populations grow as well. Migration has played an important role in accelerated urban growth. Consequently, this results in transfer of rural poverty to urban areas. Rural migrants are attracted to the urban areas for economic reasons regardless of the fact that physical infrastructure in terms of housing, drinking water supply, drainage, etc. is not so adequate in the cities. Cities have been the centers of economic growth. But planned urbanization has been ruined to an extent by the excessive demand for basic amenities resulting in deterioration in the physical environment. The quality of life has thus suffered due to continuing influx of migrants and, consequently, widening of the gap between demand and supply of essential services and other infrastructure in these areas. "Unchecked migration, especially, aggravates the housing problem resulting in an increase in the land prices. This forces the poor to settle for informal solutions resulting in mushrooming of slums and squatter settlements."[4]

Availability of land for housing is another typical urban problem. Because the poor can only afford to live in places that nobody else wants, their homes are typically in areas that have no basic infrastructure, are at risk of flooding or exposed to contamination. Furthermore, many of the urban poor do not have a legal claim to the land where they live and are at constant threat of being evicted.

The problem of urban slums has been faced at some point by almost all the major cities throughout the developing world. In many Sub Saharan African cities, the slum population accounts for over 70% of the urban population. Slums in Southern Asia, Western Asia and Sub-Saharan Africa are growing as fast as the urban population. Northern Africa is the only region in the developing world where slum growth rates have declined significantly, mainly due to the efforts of individual governments to upgrade slums or prevent slum formation. However, until other governments face this problem of urbanization with effective solutions, the global slum population is set to grow at the rate of 27 million per year between 2000-2020.[4]

II. URBAN POVERTY REDUCTION STRATEGIES: DEVELOPING COUNTRIES

Not nearly enough work has been done on urban poverty alleviation. This has been a highly ignored area among most efforts despite the fact that slum dwellers have been contributing significantly to the economy of the city by being a source of affordable labor supply for production in both the formal and informal sectors of the economy. According to the United Nations, "The world slum population of 1 billion squatter dwellers will double in the next 3 decades." Thus, comprehensive information on the slums is essential for formulation of an effective and coordinated policy for their improvement and rehabilitation as they have not received due attention in urban planning and have remained an area of neglect. Efforts to improve the lives of the urban poor have not kept up with the rate of urbanization. Running the poor out of town, through evictions or discriminatory practices, is not the answer. A lot more action is required to improve the quality of life in slums.

Helping the poor to become more integrated into the fabric of urban society is the only long-lasting and sustainable solution to the growing urbanization of poverty. While this goal seems very much out of reach, there is evidence of countries successfully reducing slum growth in the last 15 years by making considerable investments in improving slums. Some low or middle-income countries, including Brazil, Colombia, Philippines, Indonesia,

South Africa and Sri Lanka, have managed to prevent slum formation by anticipating and planning for growing urban populations by expanding economic and employment opportunities for the urban poor, by investing in low-cost, affordable housing for the most vulnerable groups and by instituting pro-poor reforms and policies that have had a positive impact on low-income people's access to services.[5] Thus, it is possible to prevent slum formation with the right policies and practices.

Colombo City: City of the Socially Excluded

Colombo is the main city and commercial capital of Sri Lanka. Within the city, the urban poor live in 1,614 under served settlements, some of which are degraded, low-cost housing, formerly owned by commercial companies and other temporary shanties built on marginalized lands[6]. The urban poor are mostly employed in the informal sector. They face social exclusion and major problems in accessing basic services. Lack of land tenure security, low incomes, poor access to clean water and sanitation, health threats due to vector-borne disease and congested surroundings, and high numbers of female-headed households are just some of the numerous problems that they face. Their community organizations are weak or non-existent, making dependency on political decision-makers the norm.[6]

Analysis of Poverty in Colombo City

With 51% of its population living in underserved settlements, the Colombo Municipal Council (CMC) has been increasingly urged to develop strategies and systems of focusing on pro-poor service delivery to the urban poor. Its first step was the creation of a poverty profile as criteria to assess poverty. The Poverty Profile was prepared through a process of dialogue with the key stakeholders. The process was bottom-up and consultative at every crucial stage. In particular, members of under served settlements were involved in developing criteria to assess poverty, carrying out the community survey, sharing primary information in the communities and developing and implementing demonstration projects. Most important of all, the CMC was able to identify that 10% of the under served settlements needed urgent, immediate attention and 40% needed considerable improvements.

UPRS for Colombo City

The Colombo Municipality, having a vision of being a caring institution responsible for the well-being of its citizens, is aiming to find a comprehensive and systematic strategy to address the urban poverty issue. Such a strategy would need to be responsive to community needs and dedicated to tackle the causes and consequences of poverty. The most important action is to make sure that each member of the Colombo community has a say in decisions impacting their lives. The only way to accomplish this is to make sure that the urban poor and vulnerable groups are included into the formal institutional structures through a process of recognition and integration. Additionally, sustainable partnerships should be developed so that resources, responsibilities and risks are shared equally among the main stakeholders. In this way, the main goal should be genuine community empowerment where resources, functions and responsibilities are shared between the urban poor and Municipality.

What's been Done?

The Government of Sri Lanka started to provide basic infrastructure in slums and shanty areas after the enactment of the Ceiling on Housing Property (CHP) Law of 1973. Housing units in slums were mostly under private ownership, but there was no proper agency to look after the shanties in the public areas when the CHP Law came into effect. Within Colombo city, about 16,000 shanty units had spread over 750 locations in 1979.[6] Shanties are illegal makeshift structures built mostly on public lands where people do not have access to basic services.

In 1979, four alternative courses of action were considered as policy by the Government in order to improve the quality of existing housing stock in Colombo: permanent upgrading; temporary upgrading; relocation on site; or relocation elsewhere. According to the Municipal Ordinance, the Colombo Municipal Council (CMC) can provide basic services and infrastructure from its own budget for the use of ratepayers only. "Even though people in slums might have been living in Colombo City for a long period of time, it was not legally possible for the CMC to provide infrastructure to these areas as people there were not paying rates to the CMC."[6]

What Went Wrong?

In many cases, the infrastructure had been built in the wrong locations. Therefore, the majority of the people in those communities did not use the amenities and were not interested in their operation and maintenance. As a result, most infrastructure built by private contractors remained unused and deteriorated quickly. During the construction stage, there was no arrangement to allow people to give their views on the design and the construction and there were delays in the commencement and completion of construction works by private contractors due to the complicated tender procedures necessary to hire them. People also complained that the cost of construction of infrastructure was high compared to their experience in building such infrastructures by themselves.[6]

Strategies to Accomplish the UPRS for Colombo

- Identify the poor urban settlements that need to be upgraded and make an assessment of constraints and limitations for extending basic amenities such as water, sanitation, electricity, access to roads and others.
- Note the entrepreneurial capacities of the urban poor by preparing community resource profiles. Once the existing opportunities and constraints for sustainable income generating initiatives are found, an environment for promoting community enterprises must be created.
- An assessment of the land tenure status of all the urban poor settlements must be done in order to develop a system of tenure rights in respect of municipal properties.
- It is very important to identify the key stakeholder groups such as CBOs, NGOs, private sector and other groups who could contribute resources and share responsibilities of implementing the different programs of the strategy.

In order to obtain the stakeholders' active participation and support in program implementation, awareness raising programs must be conducted so they understand why their help is needed.[6]

Indonesia's Urban Poor

Indonesia has adopted a liberal definition of poverty that could embody all the characteristics of poverty manifestations. The poor are indicated by basic needs deprivation, unproductiveness, inaccessibility to social and economic resources, vulnerability and no freedom.[7] Over the last 3 decades, the Government of Indonesia has undertaken many initiatives to reduce poverty through various policies and programs with the main objectives to provide basic needs such as food, education and health services, job opportunities, business credit to the poor and infrastructure assistance for urban slums. However, despite the many initiatives' success to reduce the number of poor, these programs failed to substantially solve the very basic problem of poverty. With the implementation of local autonomy in 2001, "Poverty reduction was carried out in a decentralized system by continuously encouraging the active role of local governments and communities to ensure that poverty reduction is implemented through a comprehensive, integrated and sustainable framework."[7]

UPRS for Indonesia

a. Urban Poverty Program (P2KP)[7]

- Empower local communities to assist urban residents to overcome poverty.
- Provided funding for sustainable economic activities demanded by the community groups themselves.
- Strengthened the capability of local agencies to assist poor communities.
- Encouraged broader participation in decision-making about community matters and provide equal opportunity to men and women.

b. PDM-DKE[7]

Implemented in urban areas to address income generation by using the community-based approach, which transferred funds directly to the communities affected by the Economic Crisis.

- Generated wider spread of employment and income amongst those hardest hit by the crisis and improved the socio- economic infrastructure to strengthen local economics across the entire country.

Objectives[7]

- Direct funding allocation to local governments based on levels of unemployment and poverty in the communities.
- Get local community organizations to plan, implement and manage the projects, with support from local governments.
- Rehabilitation of infrastructure and development of small and medium-scale private sector activities.

Implementation

- Funds are disbursed in the nearest banks or other financial institutions and accessed directly by the community groups.
- Project enlists the support of a wide range of local management consultants and facilitators to speed up project implementation
- Facilitators are provided at the village levels to assist project beneficiaries in planning and management.

Sustainability[7]

- Generation of jobs and stimulation of economic activity are aimed at enhancing short-term purchasing power of beneficiaries and, at the same time, help establish necessary conditions for long-term economic recovery and development.
- Program attempts to provide a link between the crisis and recovery periods to enhance sustainability of local efforts.

Criticisms

While many new initiatives on poverty reduction have been undertaken, relatively limited efforts have been done in identifying and obtaining a deep understanding of those initiatives in terms of defining and measuring poverty, selecting the approach and the target groups and evaluating its impact. Though participation of the poor is one of the main targets of the PAP, without improved capacity it is difficult to see communities participate in the programs.

UPRS for Indonesia — Balikapapan

Balikapapan has the lowest poverty rate in Indonesia, only 10% of its population is below the poverty line, however, they still have an innovative poverty program that requires the 90% well-off population to support the 10% poor population.

The vision of the city is to establish itself as an industrial, trade, service and tourism centre in the context of a 'moral' city. City's goals are to improve their human resources and provide accessible services that are environmentally friendly[7].

Policies for Poverty Alleviation[7]

- The program should not create dependency on aid.
- The program should improve the social and economic structure of the poor.
- The poor should be treated as subjects rather than objects.
- Program should involve all parties including the well-off population.

Special Poverty Alleviation Programs

a. *The 'Nine Carry One' Program[7]*

   - Means that every nine better-off people should support one poor person through mainly donations.
   - Municipal government issues a social security ID card for the poor, which entitles them to obtain health, education and other subsidies.
   - The system is managed at the district levels to ensure that assistance reaches the target groups.

- The card is meant to empower the poor by building their self-esteem rather than their dependency on charity.

Lessons Learned

a. *Engagement*

- Success of poverty alleviation depends on the active engagement of relative stakeholders and the local community.
- Building awareness of the seriousness of the problem of poverty is necessary in order to engage the local community and make everyone aware that tackling the problem of poverty was an effort that should be shared.

b. *Funding*

- When the majority of the city population is from the middle to upper-middle income bracket, it is possible to gain support and finance from the public to support any poverty alleviation program.
- In cases where poverty is a major problem, it is necessary to gain support of NGOs and donor agencies.

c. *Changing Paradigms*

- Building awareness of local stakeholders to participate in poverty alleviation programs depended on the willingness of the government to change their ways of thinking and approaching the problem of poverty.
- For example, Balikapapan did not readily accept the standards/criteria set up by the government in defining the poor. Instead, they employed a local university to conduct another study on poverty and combined the results with the government standards for their program[8].

d. *Comprehensiveness*

- While economic empowerment was the main focus to alleviate poverty, the programs were implemented comprehensively with other programs such as health, food, support, infrastructure and house upgrading and education.

Phnom Penh's Urban Poor

Over the last 10 years, rapid growth has taken place around Phnom Penh. This city suffered much neglect during the 2 decades of civil war and continues to deal with several urban problems such as overcrowding, poor infrastructure and weak institutions. In the last 2 decades, Phnom Penh has experienced unexpected in-migration of the poor with no means of livelihood in the rural areas. A survey conducted in 187 areas of Phnom Penh in 1994 estimated that urban poor communities make up 15% of the city's population of 1.1 million. The urban poor are a growing lower class composed of cycle-drivers, garbage pickers, street children and sex workers. Less than 50% of the children attended school, only 36% of the households had a sanitary toilet, 38% had poor access to water supply and 68% had no solid waste collection service.[9]

The Participatory Poverty Assessment (PPA) prepared by the Asian Development Bank (ADB) for Cambodia recognized the urban poor as being among the most vulnerable groups in the country as they are constantly exposed to violence, criminals, drug abuse and HIV/AIDS in addition to the habitual threats of insecure livelihoods and a degraded environment. Poverty, social changes and weak laws have resulted in the large-scale exploitation of women who make up 53% of the labor force and 25% of the household heads in the aftermath of the civil war.[9]

The Municipality to the Rescue

The Royal Government of Cambodia and the Municipality of Phnom Penh lacked the financial and human resources to provide a minimum of basic services to most of its citizens. The poor were clearly most affected by this situation. Most basic services and goods needed by the urban poor (water, education, health care and security) were only available in the market at a price they could not afford. Thus, these goods are unattainable for the poor either because they are unaffordable, their quality is below standard or they are purchased with borrowed money.[9]

What's been Done?

In 1998, the Phnom Penh Urban Poor Communities and Municipality Development Project organized a Strategic Planning Workshop with participation by many urban stakeholders, including the urban poor. This workshop succeeded in coming up with a base for a UPRS that would cover three broad areas: access to basic services, income generation and improved local governance.

a. *Income Generation*
   - Education, vocational/business skills, business credit, saving habits, home economics, industrial employment, marketing information.

b. *Improved Local Governance*
   - Community organization and leadership, community development councils, low-income land and housing policies, simplified procedures for government services, elimination of corruption, security of tenure.[9]

This Project also concluded that the urban poor have a large potential for individual and community-based self-improvement if:

- Strategic support is provided in terms of education, training, credit, security and technical advice.
- Legal, procedural, financial and practical barriers to self-improvement by the urban poor are removed.
- Partnerships are developed between urban poor communities and other urban actors (government, NGOs, private sector) based on mutual respect.
- Decisions on policies and programs affecting the urban poor are made at the lowest possible level of government and in close consultation with those affected by policies.[9]

The UPRS for Phnom Penh: Objectives

a. *Adequate Living Conditions for the Urban Poor*
   - Pro-poor government policies on land, low-income housing, physical infrastructure, social infrastructure, income and employment generating activities.

- Programs and projects by the municipality and NGOs that support the development of land, housing, physical infrastructure and social infrastructure by and for the urban poor.
- Government regulations and procedures that support rather than obstruct the development of land, housing, physical infrastructure and social infrastructure by and for the urban poor.
- Community construction contracts, low-income housing finance, housing advisory services, technical training programs for infrastructure and housing construction, training programs for small-scale contractors.[9]

b. *Adequate Economic Opportunities*

- Vibrant urban economy with employment opportunities in the formal and informal sector and information about these opportunities for skilled urban poor women and men.
- Vocational and entrepreneurial skills for urban poor men and women and widely known training and apprenticeship programs.
- Government regulations and procedures that support rather than obstruct the development of employment and income- generating activities by and for the urban poor.
- Micro- credit funds for micro-enterprises in the formal and informal sector and widely available information about the funds.
- Market information on the demand for and supply of goods and services for micro-enterprises in the formal and informal sector.
- Physical urban space for micro-enterprises operated by the urban poor.[9]

c. *Improved Local Governance*

- Formal or informal community organizations formed on a voluntary basis and without discrimination.

- Democratically formed, government-recognized, effective and accountable community development council representing the urban poor community and with trained community leaders.
- Special interest groups of urban poor families or persons to represent their particular interests.
- A network for the dissemination of information relevant for community organizations, community development councils, urban poor special interest groups and individual urban poor families and persons.
- Recognition by the different urban actors of the complementary roles, responsibilities and contributions of the urban actors.
- Institutionalized collaboration between community development councils, NGOs, municipality for the improvement of living conditions of urban poor communities.[9]

d. An Effectively and Efficiently Operating Municipality

- Adoption of a policy of decentralization of decision-making to the lowest possible level.
- Financial autonomy and adequate financial resources through local taxes, fees and charges for the municipality.
- Formulation, adoption and enforcement of urban plans for the development of the city of Phnom Penh that can serve as a framework for the improvement of the living conditions of the urban poor.
- Create units within the municipality to implement the urban poverty strategy.
- Adequate human resources capable of implementing the UPRS effectively and efficiently by formulating specific policies, programs and projects.
- Adequate human resources to participate in, guide, supervise and regulate the implementation of physical improvement projects, and to monitor and report on urban poverty trends in its geographical area.

- Management information service with the capacity to monitor trends in urban poverty, to assess the performance of municipal staff and departments in urban poverty reduction and the evaluation of urban poverty reduction programs and projects.[9]

Adequate Living Conditions

A strategy to develop adequate living conditions for urban poor communities in Phnom Penh should include the following policies:

Security of Tenure

Many urban poor families are forced to regularly pay protection money because of the fear of eviction. Thus, providing secure tenure is the most important component in improving the living conditions of the urban poor. Secure tenure can range from full land ownership to a temporary use right. However, secure tenure, in any form, will take away the fear of the families that they can be displaced at any moment and will, therefore, be an incentive for them to make small or large investments in the improvement of their houses.

Neighborhood Improvement

The lack of basic infrastructure (water supply, drainage, sanitation) in urban poor communities immediately affects the living conditions of the residents. The community and municipality must work together to build basic infrastructure through community construction contracts. If some funding is available, the community can carry out the construction work needed.

Housing Improvement

If secure tenure is provided and basic infrastructure can be built, it is left to the families to improve or re-build their own homes. They are capable of doing this independently but can also hire a small contractor to do it for them. Some families may need technical help regarding the construction of their new house; this can be provided by an NGO or by architecture students. In addition, many families need a small housing loan from a housing fund to finance the construction or improvement. Urban communities should be encouraged to start saving for housing improvement before the housing loan is granted.[9]

Necessary Relocation

In some cases, urban poor communities will not be able to stay and build homes where they are because their land is needed for other purposes or the settlement does not have any room for improvement. Relocation can create many problems for the urban poor such as loss of assets and income. Thus, if an urban poor community must be relocated, the community should have the chance to find a new plot of land, and since this is not always possible, the municipality should set aside land for the relocation of urban poor communities. As a result, the municipality needs to have a land policy and a plan for the city that identifies land for housing the urban poor.

Conclusions Drawn

The municipality should create conditions in which other groups can work best. It should formulate plans for the development of the city and the management of urban land so that on-site improvement and relocation of urban poor communities become part of a broader and longer-term plan[9]. It should promote the urban economy so that employment is created for the urban poor. It should create conditions for factories of multinational companies and for micro-enterprises of the urban poor to prosper for the benefit of the city population. In order to plan, the municipality should monitor social, economic and physical trends and conditions in the city. Very important is for the municipality to have qualified staff to undertake these new tasks and it needs funds to pay such staff, run its offices and make new investments. In summary, the municipality needs greater financial autonomy.[9]

III. URBAN POVERTY: A PROBLEM IN DEVELOPED COUNTRIES AS WELL

Spain— Sound Economy: No Urban Poverty

Spain has a population of about 40,000,000 inhabitants. In spite of its sound economy and wealth, urban poverty is still a serious problem. Spain has undergone increasing levels of urbanization over the past quarter century, resulting in three-fourths of the population living in urban areas. From the 60s on, Spanish cities were the target for workers with lower qualification. This situation attracted people from rural areas who migrated to cities in search of better opportunities. The rural migrants were families with little education and skills. This urbanization process increased rapidly since the introduction of the democratic constitutional monarchy system in 1978. The trend of urban growth has continued to the present time. 1999 data indicates that 77% of the total population of 39.4 million was living in urban slums.[10]

Social Exclusion

Poverty in Spain is perceived as a variable part of the wider concept of social exclusion. Social exclusion is a concept that refers to a wider, more complex problem, more related to marginality. Socially excluded people have no access to employment and other social, educational, cultural and political possibilities and chances. Despite Spain's rapid economic development since the new constitution of 1978, social exclusion still prevails. Thus, although Spain is classified as a high-income country with a gross national per capita annual income of US $14,000, social exclusion exists in the form of the marginalization of various sectors of the population.[10] However, this factor of social exclusion is not taken into consideration when calculating the poverty line. The poverty line in Spain is based on the income needed to satisfy basic 'minimum' needs and is measured in economic terms by a household's income per year—50% below the average income.[10]

Although poverty in economic terms has decreased in Spain, social exclusion is reported to have increased during the past 20 years. As a result, a significant sector of the population is marginalized outside the formal economy. The regions having communities of socially excluded people also have the *highest levels of relative poverty* suffering degradation through lack of job opportunities, inadequate housing, unstable employment and inadequate education and training, all of which create non-motivating social environments.[10]

Taking Action

However, there have been projects in Spain that tackled socially excluded groups. For example, the Housing Program for Social Integration in Navarra targeted a large portion of single parent and immigrant workers. Another project was a Program for Relocating Indigent Population in Valladold that targeted Gypsy communities. These Spanish practices relating to social exclusion attempt to help disadvantaged groups to gain access to basic shelter, infrastructure and services.

Major Housing Programs since 1978[10]

1. *The Official Protection Housing Program:* These plans were addressed to families with low income. They were simplified to make more accessible programs for families with incomes that should not exceed 2/5 times the minimum average income. Special loans at reasonable interest rates were launched to implement this program.
2. *1981-83:* This plan consisted of a housing program of 571,000 housing units addressed to lower and middle-income families. Both the private and the public sectors promoted this program. As part of this program, special loans with more flexible mortgage periods were launched.
3. *1983-87:* The transfer of power was promoted from the central government to autonomous communities; thus, shelter provision became responsibility of the regions. Also the promotion of rehabilitation and conservation of historical areas was introduced. Although most of these programs promoted the construction of substantial numbers of housing units, they were not sufficient for accommodating the poorest sectors of the society.

Government Actions[10]

National Government has also played a strong role with its financial support in relation to housing and poverty reduction programs. Between 1994 and 1999, NGO programs have received national government financial support of US $13.7 million.

Government policies and actions aimed at fighting social exclusion are:

1. State plan against social exclusion and revitalization of disadvantaged neighborhoods.
2. Drafting of an integrated action plan against marginalization (locally based and managed, by agreement between central and regional governments).
3. Active employment policy (involving local governments and relevant social actors such as trade unions, businesses, residents associations and other citizens' organizations).
4. Drafting of a general minimum income standard.
5. Drafting of a code of ethics between the political parties to implement their programs.
6. Drafting of a welcome charter for the immigration population.

Main Conclusion

The distribution of responsibilities among national, regional and local government, including NGOs in implementing these policies has been essential to ensure successful results to fight social exclusion.

Success

Many events helped the Spanish Habitat process to succeed:

1. The Spanish new political context, supported by a new constitution, allowed the formation of a constitutional monarchy and a decentralized government system of regions and local governments.
2. The people involved in the process through a powerful Habitat Committee, which was created with the support of other government and non-government institutions.
3. The role of the Habitat Committee was completely strategic as it supported the process all along by helping NGOs and municipal local governments to participate in the best practice competition.[10]

The achievements of the habitat program are a result of the competent marketing and communication campaign performed by the Committee, the University and the Ministry of Development. This efficient and comprehensive communication approach has involved all local governments greater than 10,000 inhabitants.[10]

From 1995 on, Spain experienced an immense boom in supporting international development as a result of increasing public sector and civil society interest in relation to this aspect. When Spain became a member of the EEC, it commenced development aid and cooperation programs in relation to Spanish speaking countries in South America and North Africa as well as implementing aid programs in Central and Eastern European countries.[10]

Reasons for Mass Success

An important reason relating to the success of the Spanish Habitat experience stem from the creation of a competent National Habitat Committee, which coordinated and gave support to the association of municipalities and NGOs as well as helping in writing the successive national reports. To achieve this habitat program, competent marketing and communication campaigns were carried out. This efficient and comprehensive communication approach has involved all local governments greater than 10,000 inhabitants.[10] This integration is believed to be the best way to address and eradicate poverty and social exclusion.

Main Lessons Learned

1. Use existing resources and optimize the benefits for all people affected by the specific actions.
2. Encourage a global and integral vision on existing resources by encouraging the resolution of survival problems first and ecological issues next.
3. Deal with social exclusion as a more inclusive concept than poverty.
4. Include issues of sustainability in relation to social exclusion.

5. Connect and relate the goal to local governments and neighborhood groups since they are the only ones who can best choose the most needed practices.

South Korea: An Economic Miracle?

The economic growth of South Korea has been referred to as an 'economic miracle'. In 1960, the annual per capita GNP in South Korea was US$ 69. By 1995, this figure increased to US$ 10,079. Despite this, the Korean housing situation has experienced serious problems. Given the great shortage of housing, owner-occupation has declined, rented tenure has become more common and overcrowding has become endemic. An important phenomenon to emerge has been the increasing polarization in the housing conditions of the better-off and of those of the worse-off. In 1997, Korean growth began to wane and an International Monetary Fund bail out became necessary. The impact on the economy of the crisis was severe, with the urban poor suffering more than any group[11]. The economic contraction has affected the lives of the poor in many areas and, while there are many difficult issues to deal with, the most devastating problem has been the lack of shelter for the poor.

Responses to Housing Dilemma

One of the main reasons for the housing poverty problems in South Korea has been the "inadequacy of the institutions and institutional framework for the development and management of human settlements". The term 'governance' refers to the relationship not only between governments and state agencies but also between government and communities and social groups, and means more than just government or management.[11]

In this context, effective decentralization, the efficient management of limited resources, popular participation and the development of productive partnerships between the city and the state, civil society, grass-roots communities and the private sector have emerged as essential tools in the fight waged by cities against housing poverty. Moreover, good urban governance is a prerequisite for sustainable development and the reduction of urban poverty.[11]

Three factors have helped urban governance in Korea emerge as a key issue in the discussion of policies for human settlements: democratization, decentralization and the role of NGOs.

1. *Democratization*

   The 1980s were a period of important transformation in the pursuit of a democratic political system, as well as in social development. In order to create a more democratic rule of law and administrative system, various amendments and radical policy changes were instigated. These social and political reform policies provided the foundation for the new civic government that took office in 1993. The democratic process was the result of interaction between the state, political circles and civil society, and political democratization was brought about through the efforts of a grass-roots civil society movement.[11]

Result

One important consequence of this period was the strengthening of a 'political culture' in Korea, a culture that reinforces a close relationship between political leaders and governmental institutions on the one hand; and on the other, major social and economic groups. Thus, democratic governments are more likely to operate in response to public opinion and are less likely to take arbitrary and self-serving decisions than non-democratic governments.

2. *Decentralization*

   It was not until the late 1980s that a large debate began in Korea on the issue of the balance of power and the distribution of functions between central and local governments. In 1999, the Presidential Commission on Devolution Promotion for Local Authorities was established in order to transfer powers to certain agencies of the central government. While these agencies have some autonomy in day-to-day management, ultimately the government controls them.[11]

The Presidential Commission on Government Innovation, also established in 1999, deals with the following issues:

1. Reducing the workforce and slimming down central and local government structure, with state-owned enterprises and other quasi-governmental institutions focusing on the core competencies of public functions.
2. Implementing privatization programs for state-owned enterprises and their subsidiaries, significantly increasing efficiency and performance.
3. Introducing competition and performance-oriented compensation into the public sector through such program as the Open Career System.[11]

NGOs Take Charge

"Towards the end of the 80s, sweeping change was made in Korea and democracy was enhanced as a result. This brought about an explosive growth in non-governmental and non-profit civil movements. Most existing NGOs or civil societies emerged in the aftermath of the democratic movement of 1987. Housing movements in Korea can be categorized as movements of either residents or intellectuals. Intellectuals' movements are usually composed of religious organizations and NGOs with the Citizens' Coalition for Economic Justice (CCEJ) standing out as a prominent example."[11]

The CCEJ[11]

The CCEJ believed that deep-rooted economic injustices cannot be resolved by government alone, but, ultimately, must be addressed through organized citizens' groups. CCEJ believes that the fruits of economic development should be shared by all common people and not just by a small group of 'haves'. It has proposed a new methodology of gradual, but thorough, reform on the economic system. In recognition of the need for continuous, cooperative efforts by civil society to bring about the reform of urban policies and systems, the CCEJ Urban Reform Center was established to deal comprehensively with urban problems. This urban reform movement strives to transform Korean cities into good, healthy places, based on a sustainable, environmentally friendly lifestyle.

Governing Agendas in Housing[11]

Pro-growth agendas focus on the importance of encouraging business development for a city's economic well-being and housing production. "In late 1980s, the government formulated a 5-year housing supply plan with the objective of constructing 2 million dwellings between 1988 and 1992." The government tried to address the housing problems of different income groups by employing different subsidy and finance packages, and the 2 million dwellings construction plan proved to be a success in terms of achieving mass housing production in a relatively short span of time.

"In urban areas, housing renewal projects, achieved through the demolition of sub-standard housing, were one of the crucial measures used to achieve mass housing construction and high-density development. A new style of redevelopment project, a so-called joint project, has been introduced, based on a spirit of partnership between homeowners and construction companies." This project to build high-rise flats and to share the profits was initiated on the basis of voluntary agreements between homeowners and construction companies selected by representatives of homeowners' associations. In a joint redevelopment project, the city government designates an urban redevelopment area and grants approval for all the plans; large construction companies provide the finance and carry out the construction; and an association of homeowners takes responsibility for the project.

Criticisms of Urban Renewal Projects

Although urban renewal projects, particularly joint redevelopment projects, have contributed to the supply of fairly good quality mass housing, there has been increasing criticism by some urban planners, the mass media and scores of residents concerning the collapse of community and the high-density development.[11] "If these high-density apartment construction projects fail to provide sufficient infrastructure and public services, they actually end up making the human living environment worse.

Millions of poor people, or squatters, have been evicted over the past two decades in Korea. In Seoul, 720,000 squatters were evicted, often violently, between 1985 and 1988. Most evictions concern renters who refuse to move out of the areas where they live. It has been observed that joint redevelopment projects typically involve serious human rights violations, as poor tenants are forcibly removed from their homes." In many redevelopment project areas, groups of thugs, sometimes right under the eyes of police officials, are brought in to demolish houses and force people out. Renters, who usually make up 60% of the population in redevelopment areas, are excluded by law from a share in any benefits. The economic reason for the evictions is that these projects are meant to make a profit for the developers rather than improve the quality of life of low-income tenants.[11]

Responses to Critiques[11]

One significant change that took place during the 1980s and early 1990s was the increasing influence on government actions of national and international laws concerned with peoples' right to housing. Since the early 1990s, renters evicted from urban redevelopment areas have been offered two alternatives; either receive compensation for moving expenses, usually three months' living expenses, or receive the right to move into government rental housing following construction on the project site.

Only renters excluded from compensation (because they have been residents for less than three months) or those demanding on-site temporary housing have suffered forcible eviction. Compromises are reached with about 10–20 per cent of all renters. While the first alternative may seem attractive, given the steep rises in rents in the Seoul area, the compensation offered is insufficient for tenants hoping to relocate near the redevelopment site, and thus most have to move outside of the city.

The second alternative allows residency in the same neighborhood but there is scant provision for interim housing for the four years until the project is completed. The result has been the destruction of communities. The Seoul metropolitan government has drawn up some plans to provide support for redevelopment projects initiated by communities, however, when dealing with low-income housing redevelopment, the government is faced with serious financial difficulties.

Getting the Community Involved

Community involvement agendas focus on perceived issues of social or redistribute justice and on the role of NGOs and community-based organizations (CBOs). As mentioned earlier, the majority of housing renewal projects in Korea are exploited as a means of making a profit rather than as an opportunity to improve community dynamics. As such, little consideration is given to the issues of community service, social welfare or to the advent of a total urban system. In Korea, religious organizations, CBOs and NGOs are at the forefront of citizens' housing movements.[11] Some NGOs and religious organizations have tried to establish anti-eviction campaigns and to lobby for governmental policies favorable to the urban poor. NGOs have emerged as critical intermediary institutions supporting citizens' organizations' efforts to obtain access to resources and to negotiate with local government and other state institutions. NGOs have helped form community organizations within the areas in which they are active and have responded to the needs of existing citizen groups.

The Government's Role[11]

The Korean government has played a large and increasing role in almost all aspects of housing production and consumption. A social housing program (permanent public rental dwellings) was launched at the end of the 1980s. These efforts reflect not only the acute housing shortages in urban areas but also the government's introduction of a welfare measure for low-income groups. In the late 1980s, comprehensive housing development planning was instituted to determine the extent to which national resources should be allocated to public housing development for the poor.

In 1993, the new government announced a new five-year economic plan in which, within the context of deregulation, greater emphasis was placed on the role of the private sector.

"The social housing system was abolished in early 1993 and, when compared to the previous five-year housing construction plan (1988–92), financial support for new programs for the poor continued to decline. Meanwhile, the government implemented a phased lifting of price controls on new housing in all regions, beginning in 1995, with the exception of the capital region."

Still Much More Action Needed

In Korea, existing housing policies have, in effect, not achieved their purpose. While the major objective was to increase home ownership, housing construction policy has focused on middle-income households rather than on the most needy. One important element in any future policy debate is the question of how large the public sector's role should be, as well as the question of who should produce and who should receive such housing.

How to Bring about Success?

To make the enabling process successful, the following measures need to be implemented:

1. The role played by communities regarding planning and management must be increased; in order to increase efficiency, citizens should be given more control over what happens.
2. The active participation of NGOs and CBOs at all levels will ensure legality of tenure, avoid discrimination and lead to more access to low-income housing by poor residents.
3. There must be a willingness to recognize and learn from past mistakes, so that they are not repeated. Poor residents are not looking to blame anybody for the conditions in which they live; they are only looking to improve them.
4. Linkages between neighboring residents must be maximized. The planners, residents and NGOs must work together to promote community empowerment and regeneration.
5. Finally, the experience and knowledge learned during each stage must be passed on through the efforts of staff

members and communities. The active participation of public, private and non-governmental partners should take place at all levels, to ensure legal security of tenure, protection from discrimination and equal access to adequate, affordable housing for all.

IV. INDIA'S SITUATION

India's Poverty Status

"The inadequacy of effectiveness of poverty reduction interventions in India is a critical concern." According to Bank figures (World Development Indicators 2000), India has around 433 million people living on less than US$ 1 a day, twice the number of poor in Sub-Saharan Africa, and 36 per cent of the total number of poor in the world. Poverty remains an enormous problem. Eradication of poverty is high on the development agenda of most countries; furthermore, some of them, like India, have recognized the ground reality to change the focus to poverty alleviation. Although the proportion of people below the poverty line had been declining, the trends in poverty reduction have recently worsened. Population growth is also adding to the absolute number of poor. South Asia, one of the poorest sub regions in the world, now has more than half a billion poor people, of whom 450 million are in India.[12]

What has been Done?

India's Poverty Alleviation Programmes (PAPs) are run by the Government of India, the State Governments, and the district and local authorities. The total amount spent on PAPs is 6-7 per cent of total budgetary expenditure and less than 1 per cent of GDP. Food subsidy programs make about 55 per cent of total PAP spending. The largest programs in this category is the Public Distribution System (PDS), which provides subsidized cereals and cooking medium to the poor and since 1997 is targeted to the very poor and renamed as Targeted PDS (TPDS).[12] However, due to the still increasing rate of poverty, it is evident that not nearly enough money or time has been spent on urban poverty alleviation.

Changing the Policies

In response to the growing poverty incidences in India, the "Ministry of Urban Development prepared a draft policy that was discussed at the Urban Development and Housing Minister's Conference." The earlier housing policy of 1988 aimed at providing 'adequate' shelter to all, as compared to this policy that aimed at providing 'access' to shelter for all. It recognized the shortfall in the government's efforts to provide housing and therefore, invited the private sector to actively participate in facilitating access to housing through various fiscal and other incentives. The new policy treated housing on par with infrastructure. It introduced a National Shelter Fund (set up for housing the urban poor) and a Risk Fund (to cover risks in financing the rural and urban poor). It also recognized the needs of single and working women with regard to housing.[12]

Another shift in policy was "recognition of the poor outside of slums or squatter colonies to include pavement dwellers, street children and other homeless people. This shift was facilitated by the fact that people who were above the poverty line and had the financial ability to buy many public amenities occupied several slums, especially in metros. The government began to recognize the plight of footpath dwellers and other homeless people, but acknowledged its own limitations in housing this population." Initially housing schemes aimed at providing only one-room tenements to slum dwellers and the poor, but gradually the schemes included simpler shelters.

Table 4.2[13]: Urban Slum Settlement Populations in India

Sl. No.	Type of settlement approx.	Population in lakh (2000)
1.	J.J. Clusters	20.72
2.	Slum Designated Areas	26.64
3.	Unauthorized Colonies	7.40
4.	Resettlement Colonies	17.76
5.	Rural Villages	7.40
6.	Regularised-Unauthorised Colonies	17.76
7.	Urban Villages	8.88
8.	Planned Colonies	33.08

The Five-Year Plans[14]

Since India's independence, the approach to poverty alleviation has taken shape through the five-year plans. The first four five-year plans (1951-1973) were based on economic development, equity and justice.

The Fifth Plan[14]

The Fifth Five-Year Plan (1974-79) finally addressed poverty removal as a principal objective. It did not create any special strategy for poverty removal but rather aimed to reduce its incidence through the economic growth processes and programs such as the Minimum Needs Program and public distribution of essential goods.

What Went Wrong?

The Fifth Plan did not make a distinction between rural and urban poverty. This is potentially a major reason why it was not able to make many significant changes with regards to the urban poor. Poverty changes from place to place and across time. Urban and rural areas in a given country require different measures to determine poverty levels. For example, food staples tend to be more expensive in urban areas. So the urban monetary poverty line should be higher than the rural poverty line. This is why it is so important to understand and note the difference between urban and rural areas.[15]

The Sixth Plan

The Sixth Plan recognized the limits of the 'income growth' approach to poverty alleviation. It placed 'poverty reduction' on high priority and emphasized identification and measurement of poverty issues, development of realistic targets and creation of specific programs to meet targets. An integrated approach in terms of interventions for sustainability was made through the Integrated Rural Development Program, which laid the foundation for a direct attack on urban poverty by establishing the centrally sponsored program, Environmental Improvement of Urban Slums (EIUS) for slum improvement and upgradation. EIUS worked towards moving 6 million urban poor above the poverty line through provision of extra consumption benefits, access to better and more equitable distribution of health, education, sanitation and water in addition to slum improvement and environmental improvement programs.[14]

The Seventh Plan

The Seventh Five-Year Plan (1985-90) made the first conscious attempt to directly address urban poverty. It explicitly noted the growing incidence of poverty in the urban areas and the rapid growth of slums caused by persistent rural-urban migration and overcrowding in relatively unskilled and low paid jobs in the informal sector. The Plan proposed multi- pronged strategies for provision of employment opportunities, raising earnings of low-paid jobs, and improving access of urban poor to basic services such as education, health care, sanitation and safe drinking water.[14]

The Eighth Plan

The Eighth Plan involved expansion of employment opportunities and increased productivity and income levels of both the unemployed and underemployed. It worked to achieve sustainable employment by integrating existing employment programs with sectoral development programs. Existing special employment programs were enhanced upon to initiative short-term employment for unemployed and underemployed in rural areas. This induced a reduction in the dependence on the administration for development.[14]

The Ninth Plan

The Ninth Plan identified the importance of basic services in poverty alleviation and placed major emphasis on basic services (safe drinking water, primary health facilities, universal primary education, nutrition to school children, shelter for the poor, road connectivity for all villages and habitations, and the Public Distribution System). This Plan utilized the help of PRIs, voluntary organizations and community-based Self Help Groups in the process of poverty eradication and economic growth.[14]

Criticisms

While all of these five-year plans entailed a wide range of experiments, from macro level to micro level, regional development to settlement development, a combination of re-distributive policy and individual income development and access to infrastructure, they were still lacking some key components.[14] First of all, the approaches lacked consistency and secondly, there was no direction for sustainability in the program outputs. In addition, the claim the approaches had of being integrated ended up being a combination of disjointed components of accepted anti-poverty programs and even worse, they were monitored only in terms of numerical target achievements. Thus, despite a decline in the poverty rates, there was no account of the poor population in and around the poverty lines.

Environmental Improvement of Urban Slums (EIUS)

Started in the early 1980s and initially funded by the Government of India, the aim of the program was to improve the living conditions of the slum dwellers, with a provision of basic facilities such as water supply together with drinking water taps, proper drainage system, community bathrooms and latrines, widening and adequate cleaning and maintenance of roads and street lights. The Government of India provided special monetary support of Rs. 525 per slum resident in a city with population of more than 3,00,000 people. During the early phases of this program, nearly 9.4 million slum dwellers benefited from the program and another 9.8 million during 1985-90, as per official estimates.[16]

A Step in the Right Direction

The Environmental Improvement of Urban Slums (EIUS) program was started in 1972 to provide physical infrastructure and improve living conditions. EIUS marked a change in the attitude of policy makers towards the slum population. It made a token recognition of slum dwellers as active players in the urban economy. Recognition of their own space in slums was a big leap forward for the slum dwellers. Earlier, migrants to the cities and slum dwellers had been seen as people who were encroaching on the space of established citizens. This program legitimized squatter settlements, even if they were on public land, by providing them with infrastructure facilities.[16]

Still Not Enough

The Scheme did not generate the active interest of the slum community since it did not involve them in the process of identifying specific work programs to be undertaken. As a result, the community did not have an ownership approach to the infrastructure created through the scheme and expected the municipal authorities to maintain them. However, the municipal authorities had granted de facto security of tenure, which gave rise to a sense of ownership to the residents since provision of services by the municipal government is perceived as an act of recognition of the poor. A large percentage of slum dwellers upgraded their shelter as a result of improved access to services and reduced fear of eviction. However, due to the absence of a properly designed monitoring system, there is no account of the nature of benefits received by the slum dwellers.[16]

Urban Basic Services for Poor (UBSP)

Launched in 1986, the UBSP is one of the best-designed programs of the Government of India and has covered over 10 million urban poor in 296 cities in 25 States and 6 Union Territories. Basic social services are provided such as, non-formal education, health care, nutritional supplements, and activities are also undertaken for promoting communal harmony, national integration and civic consciousness.[16]

A Multi-Sector Success

"UBSP's target was 14 lakh poor urban households or 70 lakh beneficiaries in 500 towns by 1996. The Indian government claims that UBSP integrates many other policies and paradigms of the government like the 74th Constitutional Amendment Act, National Plan of Action for Children, Convention of the Rights of the Child, Universalizing Primary Education, UN Social Development Summit. The initiation of the Urban Basic Services and 20-point program in 1986 marked a change in the perception of urban poverty." From being viewed as a single sector problem of housing, urban poverty began to be perceived as a multi-sector problem.[16]

Swarna Jayanti Shahari Rozgar Yojana (SJSRY)

The SJSRY was launched during the Ninth Plan. The key objective was to provide employment opportunities to the urban poor and the jobless by encouraging them to set up self-employment ventures or by providing different possibilities of wage employment. "The funding pattern is based on 75:25 ratios between the Government of India and the State Governments.[16] A unique characteristic of SJSRY is that it was to be based on community empowerment and in this respect the program was different from the others."

Urban Self Employment Program (USEP)[16]

The USEP, component of SJSRY, is implemented in all urban towns with particular stress on urban poor clusters, with the objective to support the urban poor in starting self-employment enterprises. The USEP also offered assistance to the urban poor women in a group of at least 10 to set up their self-employment ventures by selecting an economic activity according to their skills, training, and the local market conditions and demand. The objective is not only to generate income but also to make the women independent.

An Innovative Strategy to the Rescue

This innovative Indian poverty alleviation strategy is based on the principle that to address poverty effectively, the strategy has to be responsive, inclusive and dynamic, taking into perspective the emerging new dimensions of poverty in a functionally integrated manner.

Integrated Urban Housing Strategy: Experiences of a Secondary Town, Alwar

The strategy that was developed for this project by Society for Development Studies (SDS) seeks to provide an alternative route to poverty reduction that breaks the tentacles of dependency, builds the capacity of the community through access to information and replaces targets with sustainable impact. An indicator of the success of this approach is non-dependency of the community on public agencies or NGOs for managing their own affairs.

a. Objectives

The objective was to reduce urban poverty in a sustainable fashion through the routes of income and housing, the two MOST important voids in the lives of the poor. The uniqueness of the project is that both income upgrading and housing improvement were achieved with the same groups of households; which is not usually the case.[16]

b. Reason for Success

This brings out the inadequacy of most strategies, which only provide secure tenure and access to housing credit for the poor, without being accompanied by income enhancement strategies. This strategy demonstrates the major importance of generating a substantially higher income level in a sustainable manner if the project objective of housing upgradation is to be achieved.

National Slum Dwellers' Federation and Mahila Milan, Mumbai

The National Slum Dwellers' Foundation aimed to find workable solutions for housing of the pavement dweller community in Mumbai. The approach entailed women pavement dwellers being brought together as a group to develop a lobby for negotiating with local and state governments over a wide range of issues that affected them. The strategy sought to empower women to find their own solutions through negotiations with service and support providers.[16]

a. Objectives

Capacity building in key operational areas that concerned the development and empowerment of the women was a key component. Public meetings were arranged to discuss critical issues such as demolitions and evictions, and to work out strategies to deal with them. The next step was to develop alternative shelters, which was a challenge due to the unavailability of land. While vacant stretches of land were identified in the development plan of the city, they were not officially available to the poor.[16]

b. Steps Taken

One woman was chosen from every 15 houses and together, they formed Area Committees. They conducted regular meetings with the members of the 15 houses and acted as a link of communication among them, with the group and the rest of the community. This proved to be a powerful tool to mobilize people as the women got a sense of accomplishment and boost in their confidence. The women attended training programs, which involved analyzing their own lifestyles and their means and resources to arrive at a relevant dwelling and settlement design. "During the programs, they developed prototype dwellings with professional help. As a result, the women were ready to build full-scale model dwellings. They learnt about building materials, were trained in construction techniques, started saving money for their future homes and have been negotiating with the state authorities for land—the most valuable and scarce urban resource."[16]

c. Outcomes

This program has resulted in the organization of women pavement dwellers of Bombay and the articulation of their shelter needs. It has demonstrated that pavement dwellers have the capacity to not only save to provide for their housing but also to provide tangible inputs into the design and construction of their homes. Now there are 600 families living on the pavements in Central Mumbai who have been encouraged to save. Over the years they have managed to put aside Rs. 1,600,000, which they use whenever they need small loans to overcome a crisis. About 1,800 individuals have been given loans for various productive purposes by using external lines of credit, and each family has saved about Rs. 5000 towards their future housing.[16]

V. RECOMMENDATIONS

According to Amartya Sen, poverty alleviation policies should be expanding people's opportunities to pursue their goals. Many initiatives towards alleviating poverty have been made, however, there is not a deep enough understanding of these initiatives in terms of defining and measuring poverty, selecting the approach and target group and evaluating its impact.

UPRS for India Must Take the Following Recommended Steps:

1. The inadequacy of most poverty reduction strategies is that they only provide secure tenure and access to housing credit for the poor without addressing any form of sustainable income enhancement strategies. Urban poverty is a multi- sector problem and thus, it needs to be viewed and treated as a multi-sector problem. UPAIs need to consist of a combination of sustainable income and employment generation in addition to provision of access to basic amenities and guaranteed tenure security.[17]
2. Urban poverty reduction strategies require the collaboration of many different groups in the city— the municipality, urban poor communities, private sector and NGOs. The urban poor can build their own houses and basic infrastructure, with some external assistance. Many goods and services needed by the urban poor are available in the formal and informal private sector in the market, but they are expensive. Many NGOs have the expertise and commitment to assist urban poor communities to help improve themselves. The role of the municipality is to create conditions that make it easier for the other groups to make their contributions.[17]

   Thus, each group should do what it does best without making the urban poor dependent upon their help. Any UPRS should help the municipality, urban poor communities, NGOs and the private sector to work together better and more effectively to reduce urban poverty.
3. It is crucial that UPAIs are dedicated to mobilizing the poor towards achieving self-sufficiency rather than helping the poor to the extent that they become dependent on the program. Programs should be designed so that after a given amount of time, the target group will be in control

of their own lives and will not be in need of the program any longer.

4. Programs need to recognize slum dwellers as active players in the urban economy. This will entail discontinuation of seeing slum dwellers as 'encroachers' and instead, acknowledging them as rightfully owning the space in slums by providing them with infrastructure facilities.
5. Any decisions made by the alleviation program must be done in consultation with the slum community before implementation. It is common for many leaders of UPAIs to impose their values or beliefs of what is the 'best' for the poor without asking the poor what they think they need or if they even want help in the first place.
6. Empowerment is a term used very frequently and liberally by a majority of UPAIs without being thoroughly defined and understood. Empowering poor communities does not simply mean giving them opportunities that will falsely make them 'feel' as if they are subjects of change when they are actually recipients of aid becoming 'objects of charity'. The most important aspect of empowerment is to enable communities to be in control of their own lives. However, this cannot be accomplished if the UPAI, first of all creates a dependency of the poor upon aid and does not involve the participation of the poor in major decisions affecting them.
7. UPAIs are identical across the country since it is misunderstood that the urban condition is the same everywhere. However, there are several differences in climactic conditions, culture, resources, goods and services. Thus, each target urban area must be thoroughly studied and analyzed before any programs are implemented. An effective strategy to urban poverty is closely linked to having a good urbanization strategy.
8. UPAIs must be dedicated to achieving sustainable development. According to Carney, sustainable poverty elimination will be achieved only if external support focuses on what matters to people, understands the

difference between groups of people and works with them in a way that is congruent with their current livelihood strategies, social environment and ability to adapt.

9. Assessing the impacts and monitoring project results are necessary to understand if the programs reach intended beneficiaries, if resources are being spent efficiently, or if the program or project can be better designed to achieve the intended outcomes. Monitoring and evaluation provide direct feedback for policymakers and practitioners to design better and more efficient projects to yield better results. At the design and implementation stages, beneficiaries need to be included in monitoring the results whenever possible.[18]
10. Organizers of a UPRS must refrain from using loaded words without defining them and make sure they understand implications of such words as: democracy, empowerment, participatory, pro-poor growth, etc. It is common for stakeholders to commit themselves to 'empowering' the poor and creating 'participatory' policies. However, since policy implementers do not define these words, they are very unaware of how much work such goals will require and all the problems remain unsolved. Here is an alternative plan:
    a. First, lay out all the variables that require consideration in the UPRS such as: empowerment, democracy, decentralization, participatory governing, capacity building, etc.
    b. Then, define and decide how much work each of these goals will take and whether such goals are even realistic given resources and time constraints.
    c. Choose all realistic goals and decide how plans can be implemented to put each goal into action.

A New Paradigm Needed

The adoption of a new and innovative strategy to urban poverty is imperative. Such a strategy would require integration of multiple stakeholders to have a sustainable impact on the poor. The reason for this is that urban centres have multiple stakeholders. While the government has been making all decisions since the country's Independence, citizens are the permanent stakeholders and the most affected by the quality of these decisions. In Democracies throughout the world, the trend is shifting towards partnership with the community in the decision-making process, in recognition of the centrality of the citizen. Thus, a multi-stakeholder approach entails a collaboration of urban poor communities, NGOs, municipalities and the private/public sector. Of course, such a goal requires changing the mindsets of the three primary types of stakeholders: the government, the experts and the citizens themselves, and establishing institutional arrangements for such partnerships to succeed. This will enable addressing the key causative factors of urban poverty including income poverty, health and education poverty, personal and tenure insecurity, and disempowerment. Most importantly, countries need to get on a path of sustainable, pro-poor growth that provides opportunities for all, a voice in decision-making and protection from shocks.

Looking at the Non-Income Dimensions of Poverty

Work on non-income dimensions of poverty — defining indicators where needed, gathering data, assessing trends — is presented in the *World Development Report (WDR) 2000/01: Attacking Poverty.* This work includes assembling comparable and high-quality social indicators for education, health, access to services and infrastructure. It also includes developing new indicators to track other dimensions — for example risk, vulnerability, social exclusion, access to social capital — as well as ways to compare a multi-dimensional conception of poverty, when it may not make sense to aggregate the various dimensions into one index.[18]

Footnotes

1. http://www.globalissues.org/TradeRelated/Poverty.asp
2. World Bank http://www.worldbank.org
3. World Bank http://www.worldbank.org/html/extdr/extme/G8_poverty2000.pdf
4. http://www.indiatogether.org/2003/sep/pov-upairev.htm

5. World Bank
6. *Urban Poverty is Increasing: Colombo City.* http://www.unescap.org/pdd/prs/ProjectActivities/Ongoing/Best%20practice/Contracts%20System.pdf
7. *Innovative Approaches to Poverty Reduction: Experiences of India and Indonesia.*
8. *Ibid.*
9. *Urban Poverty Reduction Strategy for Phnom Penh.* UNDP/UNCHS. Municipality of Phnom Penh
10. *Country Report: Spain.* http://www.wmin.ac.uk/builtenv/maxlock/CityPoverty/LHA/AnnexG_%20fin16.05.02.pdf
11. *South Korea Poverty Report.* Hhttp://eau.sagepub.com/cgi/reprint/16/1/139.pdf
12. World Bank
13. delhiplanning.nic.in/Economic%20Survey/Ecosur2001-02/PDF/chapter14.pdf
14. http://planningcommission.nic.in/plans/planrel/fiveyr/welcome.html
15. World Bank
16. *Innovative Approaches to Poverty Reduction: Experiences of India and Indonesia.*
17. India Together
18. World Bank.org

References

Baharoglu, Deniz and Christine Kessides. *Urban Poverty.*

Diana Mitlin. *Understanding Urban Poverty: What the Poverty Reduction Strategy.*

http://eau.sagepub.com/egi/reprint/16/1/139/pdf

Urban Poverty Alleviation Initiatives and the JNNURM: A Critical Assessment*

5

V.K. Dhar, Ruchira Sen and *Nakul Kumar*

Introduction

Poverty, as a concept, can be associated with an individual or a family. Typically, being poor implies that an individual or a household does not have adequate money so as to purchase the basic necessities. Since poor individuals or families, usually live in a poor neighborhood, poverty has a spatial dimension. Urban Poverty is a multi-dimensional concept, with the manifestations and the causes for poverty moving in a cyclical pattern. One dimension of urban poverty gives rise to another dimension and one form of deprivation gives rise to another. For example, a household with lack of adequate resources cannot send its children to school. The children without adequate literacy cannot secure for themselves sustained sources of livelihood. This would restrict them from commanding adequate resources to improve their living standards.

Urban poverty broadly has three dimensions— livelihood/ employment, health and education. The World Bank defines urban poverty as not just a collection of characteristics, which apart from other things include limited access to employment opportunities and income, inadequate and insecure housing and services, violent and unhealthy environments but also as a dynamic condition of vulnerability or susceptibility to risks.

In India, urban poverty is defined in terms of minimum calorie intake, at 2100 calories per capita per day. This is a

---

* *Courtesy*: www.niua.org.

convenient measure for identifying the urban poor for the purpose of implementing Urban Poverty Alleviation Initiatives (UPAIs). The Planning Commission's revised methodology of 1997 results in an average poverty line for India of Rs.353/- per capita per month for 1996-97. This equals approximately Rs. 21,180/- per household per annum. On this basis, Planning Commission data indicates that the urban poor were estimated to be 7.5 crores, comprising 38 per cent of the total urban population in 1988. This number rose to 7.63 crores in 1993-94, i.e. 32 per cent of the total urban population.

Urban Poverty Alleviation Initiatives in India

India has quite rightly laid an emphasis upon the elimination of poverty throughout its development plans. On the 14th of August, approaching midnight, in his historic 'Tryst with Destiny' speech, Pandit Jawaharlal Nehru reminded the nation that the "ending of poverty and ignorance and disease and inequality of opportunity" is one of the prime tasks of modern India. However, the Planning Commission realized that mass poverty could only be tackled as a part of a development strategy supported by a radical policy framework of institutional reforms. It began formulating strategies only after commissioning the first households surveys of the urban poor in 1951. The incidence of poverty was 53 per cent then and according to the 55th round of the NSS survey has currently reduced to 26.1 per cent (23.62 per cent in urban areas and 27.09 per cent in rural areas). Bihar, Madhya Pradesh, Rajasthan and Uttar Pradesh (BIMARU) account for 51 per cent of the BPL population in the country. If combined with the eastern states— Assam, Bihar, Orissa and West Bengal, the BIMARU and eastern region account for 70 per cent of the poor in the country.

There are two approaches to tackle poverty—the Indirect and the Direct 'attack'. The Indirect approach works on the principle of the trickle-down effect. It believes that a rapid growth of per capita income will benefit the poor, thus, Community Development Projects (CDP) in 1952 and National Extension Service (NES), 1953 were initialized after the First Five-Year Plan. The Direct approach is based upon the fact that "widespread poverty is a challenge which no society in modern times can afford to ignore for long". This has two components—providing livelihood via employment guarantee schemes and providing basic services like electricity, water, sanitation, primary health care, etc. which shall enable the poor to save by not spending money on generators, and the treatment of illnesses arising from poor sanitation and sewerage.

India's first initiative to eradicate urban poverty was the Subsidized Industrial Housing Scheme (SIHS) in 1952. Since then, urban poverty alleviation programmes have gathered momentum in three overlapping phases—the housing phase, 1952-1997, the welfare phase from approx 1956 to 2002 and a credit and employment phase from 1977-1997.

Government Initiatives Regarding Housing

The Subsidized Industrial Housing Scheme, which targeted the industrial workers employed in factories and mines in the public and joint sector, was responsible for the construction of 282,829 dwelling units at a cost of Rs. 1701.24 crores. Fifty per cent of the housing cost was subsidized and loans were available for the other half of the cost. Employers providing housing facilities for their workers were given financial assistance up to 75 per cent of the cost.

In 1952, a scheme for Economically Weaker Section (EWS) housing was implemented. Approximately 11 lakh plots were distributed since 1980. About 65,432 shelter units were constructed during the Sixth Five-Year Plan. Houses and plots of 25 to 30 sq mts were provided at cost price. By 1992, construction loans up to Rs. 19,500 became obtainable and so did repair loans of up to Rs. 9500. These were repayable in 20-25 years at concessional rates of interest. The Average cost of an EWS house is currently Rs. 35,000. This scheme was sponsored primarily by HUDCO, which raised almost Rs. 800 crores annually.

The Low Income Group Housing Scheme (LIGHS) came about in 1954. HUDCO allowed construction loans of Rs. 55,000 and repair loans of Rs. 37,500. The average cost of a LIG house is currently Rs. 100,000. One-third of these LIGHS houses were to be reserved for the EWS. Another important development that took place in 1954 was the formation of the Ministry of Works and Housing (MoWH), which was later renamed as the Ministry of Urban Development (MoUD) in 1985. This was bifurcated into the Department of Urban Development (later the MoUA and then the MoUD) and the Department of Urban Employment and Poverty Alleviation (later the MoUEPA). In May 2000, the Ministry of Urban Development (MoUD) and the Ministry of Urban Employment and Poverty Alleviation (MoUEPA) were merged to form the Ministry of Urban Development and Poverty Alleviation (MoUDPA).

Another important development in 1954 was the establishment of National Building Organisation (NBO), the United Nation's regional housing centre for Economic and Social Commission for Asia and the Pacific (ESCAP). This collects, processes and disseminates information related to housing and innovative construction methods.

The Slum Areas Improvement and Clearance (SAIC) Programme was launched in 1956 for Class III and IV government employees, including scavengers, gardeners and sweepers. Calcutta, Delhi, Madras, Bombay, Kanpur, and Ahmedabad were prioritized along with towns with a population of above 100,000. The Central Government provided a subsidy to the State Governments to facilitate a classification of slums into slums that must be cleared and redeveloped and slums that must be upgraded, provide separate washing platforms and provide housing and skeletal housing. Following this scheme, the Land Acquisition and Development Scheme (LADS) allowed the government to acquire land for public purposes. The Delhi Development Authority was founded in 1958. It has a 'Slum Wing' to take care of minimum amenities to be provided to the slum dwellers, upgradation, resettlement and the Environmental Improvement of Urban Slums (EIUS) according to the SAIC.

Housing and Urban Development Corporation (HUDCO) was founded in 1970 as an apex national techno-finance agency in the housing sector. It has been involved in financing the construction of EWS, LIG houses and EIUS Schemes. It is responsible for the implementation of National Housing and Habitat Policy and it has established a Habitat Polytech in New

Delhi to train NGOs and engineers in habitat planning and management.

The Minimum Needs Programme (MNP) was introduced in the Fifth Five-Year Plan initially as a Rural Poverty Alleviation Programme. By 1980, its focus shifted to urban affairs targeting landless labourers and BPL families. It provided basic minimum services like slum upgradation to include health facilities, water supply, electrification, road connectivity, housing, elementary education and nutrition. In the Sixth Five-Year Plan, adult education was also included and in the Seventh Plan, domestic energy and sanitation were provided as well. The State Governments are the implementing agencies.

In the same year, HUDCO brought out the SS-Sites and Services, targeting low-income families the monthly incomes of which do not exceed Rs. 700. Loans, sites for small businesses and low-cost housing with amenities like toilets, baths, access roads, truck water, and sewer lines.

1988 was an eventful year for urban housing The National Housing Policy was brought about by the MoUDPA to provide low-cost housing technology, appropriate materials, information and skill upgradation to artisans and footpath dwellers. The National Housing Bank was established as a subsidiary of the RBI to mobilize and channelize resources for the National Housing Policy and to refinance HUDCO and other state and local home financing institutions. The National Network of Building Centres (NNBC) was founded to create a decentralized delivery system for the training and upgradation of skills for housing technology, use of low-cost but high quality materials and those produced out of agro-industrial waste, training of local artisans and unemployed youth. By 1989, 41 centres were operational. By 1996, there were 435 centres but only 239 were operational.

The Night Shelter Scheme came about in 1988. It targeted 2 lakh footpath dwellers in 12 metros and set up 56 schemes to provide 19,366 beds, 5258 pay-and-use toilets, 64 baths and 145 urinals. It was a part of the National Housing Policy, 1988. Community night shelters with minimal sanitary and water supply, and a place to park rickshaws were constructed. The cost of construction was a maximum of Rs. 5000. The Centre subsidized Rs.1000 and the voluntary construction agency could take the rest of the money as a loan from HUDCO. For pay-and-use toilets, the Central subsidy was limited to Rs. 350 a user. This was a joint project of GoI, MoUDPA, the State Governments, the ULBs and HUDCO.

In 1990 the Building Materials and Technology Promotion Council (BMTPC) took over the functions of the National Building Organisation (NBO). An Urban Poverty Alleviation Fund was created in each municipality. The President is the Union Minister for Urban Development. It is comprised of representatives from the Union, States, NHBs, HUDCO, IDBI, IFFCO and ICICI.

In 1994, the Planning Commission's Modified Expert Group made estimates of urban poverty after modifying the methodology for calculating state specific poverty lines.

Government Initiatives Regarding Welfare

In the early years of the Welfare Phase of the poverty alleviation schemes, welfare was usually coupled with housing. The SAIC, 1956 was also an attempt to provide Basic Services to the Urban Poor. (BSUP) In 1958, welfare schemes began to gain momentum with the Urban Community Development (UCD) Programme. This was a bid to strengthen local voluntary organizations and establish basti level agencies, self-help groups and community organizations. Pre-school classes, immunization schemes, crèches, mid-day meal centres and medical check up schemes were launched. So were Mahila Mandals and income generation training programmes for women. Vocational education in terms of typewriting classes, auto rickshaw driving classes, etc. was imparted and dispensaries, study tours, basti committees, co-operatives, and anti-mosquito drives were facilitated. This was a centrally sponsored scheme but the monetary burden was shifted to the states later on. The UNICEF and the Ford Foundation also contributed substantially in terms of funds.

In 1961, the Urban Water Supply and Sanitation (UWS&S) Scheme was launched to provide good sewerage or improve the existing sewerage system. Storm water drains and feeder mains were constructed, clear water reservoirs were rehabilitated and the drainage system was improved.

The Mid-Day Meal (MDM) Programme, which was included in the Minimum Needs Programme (MNP) in the Fifth Five-Year Plan in 1974, provided supplementary nutrition as a mid-day meal in schools. It covered 20 million children by the end of the Sixth Five-Year Plan.

The Special Nutrition Programme (SNP) in 1970 followed this. It too, was a part of the MNP. It provided food supplements of 300 calories and 10 grams of protein per child, 600 calories and 20 grams of protein to severely malnourished children and 500 calories and 15-20 grams of protein to pregnant/nursing women. As can be seen, this was not a self-sustaining programme. The UNICEF assisted the Central and State Governments to tackle the financial burden. It was mainly a scheme for the delivery of services rather than for the empowerment of the poor to earn the services on their own. The same can be said for the Balwadi Nutrition Programme implemented in 1971.

In 1972, the EIUS was implemented. It was included under MNP, in convergence with the Urban Basic Services for Poor (UBSP) since 1992-93, in the National Slum Development Programme (NSDP) in 1996. Sanitary latrines, drainage, portable water supply, road connectivity and street lighting were provided. The per capita assistance to each slum dweller has been Rs. 800 since 1995. It was a centrally sponsored scheme till 1974 after which the financial burden was shifted on to the State Governments.

The Integrated Child Development Services (ICDS) Scheme was set out to provide non-formal pre-school education, early stimulation and learning, supplementary nutrition, and immunization for children. Water and environmental sanitation were also provided. Its Adolescent Girls Scheme seeks to meet the needs of 11-18 year old female school dropouts in terms of education, literacy, nutrition and skill formation. Training camps and hands-on-learning camps were organized. In 1979, the Non Formal Education (NFE) Programme was launched to cater to similar needs of other children that aren't covered by the formal education system.

The Integrated Development of Small and Medium Towns (IDSMT) was launched in 1979. It set up infrastructure and facilities for towns to serve as service centres for their surrounding rural areas. It was hoped that these would take the force of the rural-urban migration away from the bigger and more overcrowded and slum-ridden cities. Each town was given a central grant of Rs.52 lakhs with 6 lakhs to be used for Low Cost Sanitation (LCS). Since post-1995, the Centre and the State have been sharing the financial burden equally with assistance from the UNICEF.

The LCS Scheme was an attempt to convert all 50 lakhs existing dry latrines into low-cost pour-flush sanitary latrines on a "whole town" basis. The scheme was subsidized by the Central Government, supported by the UNICEF and the State Government (50:50 burden). HUDCO loans were available.

The National Health Policy (NHP) formulated in 1982, reorganized health infrastructure, improved medical and paramedical training, integrated health plans with health related sectors like water supply, sanitation, food production, etc. It recognized the role of voluntary organizations like the Rotary Club and the Lions Club.

The Universal Immunization Programme attempted to develop an extensive cold chain throughout the country for the storage of vaccines, an indigenous capacity to manufacture vaccines and to issue immunization cards to beneficiaries, thereby keeping records. The especially appointed National Technology Mission ran it.

The Urban Basic Services (UBS) Programme intends to strengthen income generating skill, training for women, early childhood learning facilities, and child crèches for children. More community taps and Mark II pumps were installed and maintained, and so were low-cost pour-flush toilets, and arrangements for garbage and sullage disposal. A *Basti* Development Committee was formed to develop mini plans and supervise and maintain facilities under UBS. The Public Health Engineering Department is to support the construction of smokeless stoves, bathing cubicles, garbage pits and drains. It was subsumed in the Urban Basic Services for the Poor (UBSP) in 1990. This integrated the social services under UBS and the physical amenities under EIUS. It created an Urban Poverty Alleviation Fund in each municipality to combine the funds for each scheme.

In the late 1980s training and employment programmes became more of a norm. The Support for Training and Employment Programme for Women (STEP) aimed at integrated development, and training and upgradation of skills in agriculture, handicrafts, small animal husbandry, dairying, fisheries, handlooms, sericulture, khadi and village industries, social forestry and wasteland development. It mobilized women in viable groups and arranged support services like health check-ups, mobile crèches, education facilities, gender sensitization and access to credit.

In 1988 the National Literacy Mission (NLM) acquired for the Kottayam district of Kerala, its famed 100 per cent literacy. It covered 556 out of 588 districts. In the same year, the National Commission for Self-Employed Women and the Women in the Informal Sector (NCSEW & WIS) did a situational review of women in the informal sector and recommended the introduction of protective measures to guarantee employment, income generation, minimum wages, and upgradation of skills.

In 1993, the Employment of Manual Scavengers and Construction of Dry Latrines (Prohibition) Act made the employment of manual scavengers a punishable offence. Kerala, Karnataka, Gujarat and Tripura declared a scavenger-free government. The Accelerated Urban Water Supply Programme targeted 215 eligible small towns with a population of less than 20,000 (1991 Census) in Class IV, V, and VI categories. It tried to improve the quality of life of the poor by reducing water scarcity, improving the revenue base of urban local bodies and improving their involvement.

In 1996, the National Slum Development Programme (NSDP) brought in upgradations in infrastructural facilities, community centres, education, housing, thrift and credit societies, water and sanitation, primary education, adult literacy, SWM, garbage disposal, etc.

In 1997, the Targeted Public Distribution System (TPDS) replaced the old PDS. It issued 10 kg of foodgrains especially rice and wheat every month to each BPL family at 40% of the cost. Non-BPL families would also be entitled to these foodgrains and edible oils, kerosene and sugar at 80% of the cost. It can be noted that BPL families can easily sell their rations to the non-BPL families in the black market. This scheme is obviously not efficient.

The Valmiki Ambedkar Malin Basti Awas Yojana (VAMBAY), 2001 tried to identify and meet the shelter needs of the urban poor. Twenty-five per cent of funds were earmarked for water supply and sanitation, and 2 per cent for making model demonstration slum upgradation projects. The scheme was under DUEPA, MoUD, HUDCO and poverty alleviation NGOs.

Government Initiatives Regarding Credit

The first Credit Scheme for the urban poor began in 1997 with the Differential Rate of Interest (DRI), originally started in 1972 but expanded to include the urban poor in 1977. Subsidized credit was given by commercial banks for 3 years. The maximum loan amount was Rs. 6500 at an interest of 4% to be repaid within 5 years, inclusive of the two-year grace period. SC/STs and the handicapped could obtain an additional loan of Rs. 5000, the former for housing and the latter for aids and appliances for an entrepreneurial venture.

The Nehru Rozgar Yojana (NRY) was launched in 1989 to target BPL urban households, 30% of which should be women headed. SCs and STs were represented in proportion to their population. Up to 10 lakh urban unemployed and underemployed poor were expected to benefit from the schemes under NRY. The NRY Scheme of Urban Micro Enterprises (NRY-SUME) set up small enterprises related to servicing and small-scale manufacturing. Training was undertaken through

ITI, and polytechnics run by the government, the private sector and the NGO sector at a per capita expenditure of Rs. 1200. Women and other beneficiaries, without collateral or a third party guarantee, may obtain a maximum of Rs. 5000 as loan. Women, SCs/STs and others, may obtain the remaining from a bank at a maximum of Rs. 15,000.

The NRY Scheme of Wage Employment for public assets creation (SUWE) was an employment guarantee to develop social infrastructure programme. Rs. 15 per day was paid to unskilled labourers and Rs. 25 per day to skilled labourers. The NRY-Scheme for Employment through Housing and Shelter Upgradation (SHASU) targeted those of the urban poor with tenure security for at least 10 years. The per capita training expenditure was Rs. 1500. HUDCO loaned Rs. 19,500 for the construction of each EWS house. This could be repaid in 10 years. Twenty-five per cent of the costs up to Rs. 1000 were subsidized. The State Government was to appoint a nodal agency, e.g. The State Slum Board for the implementation.

The Scheme of Liberation and Rehabilitation of Scavengers (SLRS) in 1993 was an attempt to provide scavengers especially the SCs and STs with alternative employment. The 50% subsidy was subject to a maximum of Rs. 10,000. Loans up to Rs. 6500/- were to be treated as DRI and were repayable in 3-7 years inclusive of the 6-month grace period.

The Prime Minister's Rozgar Yojana was an attempt to provide self-employment to the educated unemployed in the industrial, service and business sectors. Fifteen per cent of the project was subsidized subject to a ceiling of Rs.7500/- per entrepreneur and Rs.15,000 per entrepreneur in the N.E. States. No collateral was required for industrial loans below Rs. 2 lakh and Rs. 5 lakh in case of partnership projects. Service loans below 1 lakh could be obtained without collateral. Repayment ranged from 3-7 years. Training expenses were Rs. 1000 per capita.

The Swarna Jayanti Shahari Rozgar Yojana (SJSRY) was launched in 1997. It identified BPL households residing in town for at least 3 years and not having defaulted on any loan from a nationalized bank, as per state-specific poverty lines. In addition to these, other beneficiaries were identified by the following parameters: The condition of roof, floor, water, sanitation, education level, type of employment, and the status of the children in a household. It formed Neighborhood Groups (NHGs) in areas where 10-40 women lived in a neighborhood in homogeneous circumstances. One was elected as Resident Community Volunteer (RCV) to co-ordinate the activities and to act as a conduit between the NHGs and the Neighborhood Communities (NHCs). An NHC was formed of RCVs from NHGs in the same area and representatives from other community programmes. It addressed local problems through training with NGOs and CBOs—A convener was selected to represent the NHC in a Community Development Society (CDS)— a formal association of NHCs at the town level. It ensured repayment of loans and tried to build small community assets.

The SJSRY Urban Self Employment Programme (USEP) targeted the urban poor BPL in all towns, unemployed and underemployed youth, 30% of which are women, and 3% disabled. SCs and STs were represented on basis of their proportion in the population. Women headed households were prioritized. The objective of the SJSRY-USEP was to generate self-employment through micro-enterprise and skill development. Some entrepreneurial ventures would require no skills, e.g. Setting up a tea shop, laundary work, vending but some would like electronic repairs, construction works, small units, manufacturing garments, furniture, food processing, agriculture and allied business. The maximum unit cost to be incurred in setting up each unit is Rs. 50,000 per person. Fifteen per cent of the project was subsidized and the beneficiaries as cash provide five per cent. Ninty-five per cent could be obtained as a bank loan without collateral at priority sector loan interest rates. Loans were to be repaid within a period of 3-7 years after an initial moratorium of 6-18 months. The CDS was to ensure repayment. The SJSRY-USEP also tried to upgrade vocational and entrepreneurial skills, at a cost of Rs. 600 per beneficiary per month.

The SJSRY-USEP Development of Women and Children in Urban Areas (DWCUA) carried out self-employed ventures for groups of 10 women (18-60) from identified BPL families.

The SJSRY-USEP Thrift and Credit Societies (TCS) functioned as an informal bank of the poor releasing Rs. 1000 per capita for purchasing raw materials, etc. It loans a maximum of Rs. 2000 with a 2% monthly interest charge. As per the SJSRY Urban Wage Employment Programme (UWEP), it provides wage employment by utilizing labor for the construction of socially and economically useful public assets, at minimum wage rates, providing minimum infrastructure services.

The 74th Amendment

The 74th Amendment was an overall approach to eliminate poverty. It was also a very large step in democratic decentralization. It gave more power to the local bodies to participate in the development process and conducted direct elections for seats in municipalities via the State Election Commissioner appointed by the Governor. One-third of the seats were reserved for women. This amendment act included urban poverty alleviation plans, plans for slum improvement and upgradation as a legitimate municipal function. An Urban Poverty Eradication (UPE) Cell was set up in each town headed by a trained Town Project Officer under the concerned Urban Local Body (ULB). A Finance Commission was constituted at the state level to review the municipal finances every five years.

A Critical Analysis of the UPAIs

Data suggests that the UPAIs in India have had a reasonable amount of success in the targeted areas. From a broad look at the programmes it becomes clear that most of these targeted the emancipation of women and infrastructural development. While the projects in themselves were wholesome, the poverty alleviation strategy missed out on the essential aspects of urban poverty. Urban poverty has three aspects, clearly mentioned in the introduction. It is staggering to note that only a smattering of these initiatives actually targeted the creation of livelihood opportunities for the poor. Programmes like the NREGS, have come under severe stricture from different quarters. In spite of this, no efforts were made to bring about better and more polished plans for the poor or implement them in the urban areas. The Food For Work Program was restricted only to the rural areas.

This brings us to the next criticism of the UPAIs. Given that urban poverty was not recognized as a separate phenomenon until the Ninth Five-Year Plan. Most of the UPAIs were subsumed within the broader city development plans. As such specific needs of the poor were largely ignored and the development strategies were tangential to poverty alleviation. Another area that deserves focus is the housing schemes initiated by the government. It seems that they were too many in number, and thus missed out the core group. Moreover, given the number of loopholes in the system how far the targeted group benefited is rather specious. It is essential to realize that while the poor may be provided with proper living spaces, unless the surrounding areas are clean and till the poor are provided with adequate means of sustenance, such benefits cannot be sustained.

Another prime area of importance that seems to be lost in discussion is that of the informal sector. Almost 30 per cent of the economy's output is contributed by the informal sector. While individuals employed in the sector are usually considered to be better-off than those without any source of employment, the truth is that the condition of the informal workers is equally bad, or in some cases even worse. Most of them put in huge hours of work, without being rewarded appropriately. There is a continuous danger of accidents or physical injury, against which these workers are not insured. They work in inhumane conditions and stay in the worst of areas in order to be able to stay closer to the job places. No efforts have been made to rescue such workers from their pitiable conditions. City development has often blamed for the influx of migrants, and efforts have been made to reduce such migration through poverty alleviation in the villages, however there have been no efforts to target and reduce the poverty of the migrants who have already settled in the cities.

Table 5.1: Sources of Credit for the Poor

Credit Source	% of Total Credit Borrowed	Cumulative	Total Credit Availed (Rs.)	Number of Loans Taken	Average Loan Amount (Rs.)	Average Interest Rate Per Month		
						<5%	5.10%	>10%
Moneylenders and Chit Funds	53.5	(53.5)	36,36,100	429	8,475	1.2	15.9	82.5
Friends	19.5	(73.0)	21,66,300	205	10,567	17.5	21.2	61.2
Pawn Brokers	13.6	(86.6)	3,39,800	85	4,000	14.4	65.2	20.3
Relatives	6.9	(93.5)	8,71,000	63	13,825	40.9	26.2	32.7
Sangha	2.3	(95.8)	1,56,000	16	9,750	100.0	–	–
Employer/Office	1.7	(97.5)	43,400	21	2,0666	73.6	15.0	10.5
Others	1.7	(98.9)	1,45,500	13	11,192	53.8	15.3	30.7
Banks	0.8	(99.7)	1,22,000	5	24,400	100.0	–	–
Private Finance	0.3	(100.0)	–	–	–	–	100.0	–
Total	100.0		74,80,100	837	9,402			

There also seems to be much agog over the Formal Credit to the urban poor, as an essential UPAI. Statistics suggest that a majority of the urban poor are not willing to take formal credit, just to avoid the huge transaction cost. They are more than willing to pay higher rates of interest and stand to be further impoverished by this. However, they do get convenience and timely supply of credit, without having to compete for it, in return. This is despite the fact that the urban areas have scads of bank branches.

A study conducted in Bangalore by the Paradigm Group seems to justify the above case.

Thus what is needed in India is an overall integrated approach to alleviate poverty—an approach that tackles each and every identifiable problem—housing, training for a means of livelihood, employment measures and providing basic services to the urban poor. Our policymakers have tried to develop such approaches but so far, they have not been entirely successful. Even the BSUP sub mission of the JNNURM, which shall be discussed below, is hardly an integrated approach to the alleviation of urban poverty, mainly because it does not include schemes for livelihood.

The Jawaharlal Nehru National Urban Renewal Mission (JNNURM): Strategies For Poverty Alleviation

The UPAIs have brought us this far. Where next? This is broadly the question for which the BSUP sub mission of the JNNURM seeks answers. The aim of the JNNURM is to encourage reforms and fast track planned development of identified cities. Focus is to be on efficiency in urban infrastructure and service delivery mechanisms, community participation, and accountability of ULBs/Parastatal agencies towards citizens. The objectives of the JNNURM directly targeted at the urban poor, include a scale-up delivery of civic amenities and provision of utilities with emphasis on universal access to the urban poor and the provision of basic services to the urban poor including security of tenure at affordable prices, improved housing, water supply and sanitation, and ensuring delivery of other existing universal services of the government for education, health and social security.

Basic Services to the Urban Poor (BSUP) is an essential component of any poverty alleviation strategy. Consider for example an improvement in the facilities for Solid Waste Management. It is quite clear that poor sanitation in areas surrounding the residence of the poor has been a major cause of diseases like cholera, dysentery. etc. In the absence of adequate government health care facilities, the poor spend large amounts on the treatment of these diseases, and for those who cannot afford them, often watch helplessly. With proper SWM in place, the occurrence of such disease can be reduced, helping the poor save on the health care expenditure. Similarly, with health care facilities in place, the poor can save on expenditures in private health care centres. In both situations, the poor tend to save, and use the money to rise out of poverty.

A major advantage of the JNNURM is the focus on such and other similar areas to be targeted as admissible components.

As a part of the JNNURM, each of the selected 63 cities is required to prepare a City Development Plan, that analyses amongst other things the prevalent situation, with regards the urban poor, vision and strategies that the city wishes to implement, to cure the curse of urban poverty. A critical examination of ten of these CDPs gave a plethora of wide ranging results that have been summarized below. A detailed appraisal of each of the CDP is given in Annexure I-X.

The analysis of the existing scenario with regards the urban poor is largely an outcome of the above poverty alleviation initiatives that were undertaken during post-independence period. These initiatives were applied uniformly across states without recognizing the heterogeneity among them. This proved to be a limiting factor in the success of most of these initiatives. Through the CDPs, the states have now made an effort to devise poverty alleviation strategies specific to their state, based largely on the analysis of the existing situation.

Some cities have concentrated on the urban poor with regard to their development plan in commendable detail. The Vadodara Municipal Corporation has recruited SEWA, an NGO, that usually concentrates on the interests of self-employed women, especially to conduct surveys to estimate the existing condition of basic services available to the urban poor. In its stakeholder consultations, it has also taken an opinion poll of NGOs, CBOs, etc. working with the urban poor (primary stakeholders) on which of the basic services needs to be developed on a priority basis.

Other Gujarat CDPs are also noteworthy. The Rajkot Municipal Corporation has evaluated the infrastructural condition of the urban poor by considering the types of roofs, the access to water and sanitation facilities and the types of floors as indicators.

Kohima has provided a matrix enumerating in detail a profile of each and every slum with respect to population, housing type and infrastructure. The primary stakeholders have duly represented the urban poor in the stakeholder consultations.

Raipur on the other hand, hasn't analyzed the living conditions of the urban poor at all, nor in fact has Chandigarh except for a cursory mention...

However, the emphasis on BSUP of most of these CDPs, even the better ones like Vadodara, is far from perfect. Chandigarh has provided no details about the number of slums, the percentage of the population living in slums, the BPL population, etc. Raipur, Rajkot, Kohima, Vijaywada, Ahmedabad and Hyderabad have not enumerated the projected slum population in 2011. This statistics is essential in order to assess whether the facilities that shall be provided under JNNURM shall be sufficient to meet the demands of the future population.

Another drawback of many of these CDPs is that their visions and strategies for providing BSUP focus on infrastructural build-up and maintenance in the slum areas. In Kohima for instance, only 34.9 per cent of the BPL population lives in the slums. If slum areas are targeted only, 65.1 per cent of the BPL population shall not be affected at all. Similarly in Vadodara, the percentage of the BPL population exceeds the percentage of population living in the slums by 16 per cent. Therefore, it can be deduced that 16 per cent of the population is totally left out of the JNNURM sub mission to provide BSUP. In Vijaywada the percentage of population left out of the project is 9.69 per cent approx. To remedy this, squatter settlements should be targeted along with slums. At any rate, detailed estimates, perhaps by a specially recruited NGO like SEWA should be conducted to assess where the percentage of BPL population that does not live in slums lives. These areas should either be integrated or rehabilitated and be provided with BSUP.

As per infrastructural analysis, the JNNURM toolkit expects a detailed report with respect to quality, quantity and coverage. Most CDPs, however, have not dealt with quality at all. This includes Vijaywada which states the percentage of urban poor who have an access to basic facilities but does not mention the number of hours for which water is supplied, how often do the storm water drains require repairing, etc. In this context, Vadodara CDP is very well written. Also, it is important to mention the consequences of a low, indeed a less than 100 per cent access to any of the basic services. For example, consider the CDP of Ahmedabad. The CDP states that 506 households queue for one private toilet. The implications of this need to be evaluated further, those who are at the back of the queue, might be unable to wait and might perhaps defecate in the open. Thus while more community toilets should be built, the diseases that might arise from open air defecation must be identified by health camps and the people living in surrounding areas must be immunized.

Similarly, most CDPs apart from Surat and Chandigarh have enumerated the social infrastructure that even slum dwellers have an access to. However, many like Hyderabad have not provided any information on the number of students enrolled in the schools, the number of drop outs, etc.

The Vision and Strategies of the cities have been plotted and planned in an accurate and realistic manner. The only commendable aspect of the CDP of Raipur is that it recognizes the importance of developing the informal sector. Rajkot plans to issue tenure rights along with BSUP so as to ensure that the slum dwellers are not evicted due to a rise in land value caused by the introduction of BSUP.

The CDP of Ahmedabad is truly unique as a part of the funds for providing BSUP shall be provided by the slum dwellers

(Rs. 2000 per household). This shall motivate them to look after the facilities in a better manner. Cheap and easy micro-credit facilities shall be provided by SEWA.

A detailed report on how each CDP has focused on the urban poor has been provided in Annexure I-X. Annexure XI is a comparative matrix.

Root of The CDPs

With a view to encourage greater stakeholder consultation and a more pro-poor urban development strategy, the Cities Alliance[1] has propounded the concept of the City Development Strategy (CDS), which is where the CDPs stem from.

> A CDS is an action plan for equitable growth in a city, developed and sustained through public participation to improve the quality of life for all citizens.
>
> —The Asian Development Bank

Population explosion is no longer a phenomenon, unknown to the urban cities of the developing countries. A natural increase and a large influx of rural population have been inflating the population statistics. While it is expected that the population in the urban areas will double by the year 2009, the inadequacy of social and physical infrastructure is worrying the policy-makers.

The city development strategies have thus been initiated to make key decisions on urban development, with a focus on implementation.

The City Development Strategy seeks to find ways with which to improve a city's competitiveness, livability, management and financial solvency. It is a process that requires the coalition of local leaders to improve the cities' strategies, reviewing its opportunities and challenges. It is a strategy analyzed collectively and prioritized to stimulate or sustain economic growth, and bring about an improvement in the quality of urban life (World Bank).

The CDS requires the city to be clear on its vision and prepare a long-term strategy, from which short-term strategies are derived. There needs to be an all-inclusive participatory process, with a special focus on the needs of the vulnerable. Most important is that there be capacity building through a transfer of knowledge across cities.

City Development Strategies (CDS) link the process by which local stakeholders define their vision for their city and its economic growth, environmental and poverty reduction objectives, with clear priorities for actions and investments. The stakeholders assess the city's strengths and weaknesses, reflected in their aspirations for the city, and formulate a shared vision. Carrying on the CDS process through strategy formulation, selecting solutions from various options, initiating an action, a program, a project, or a policy change though is a difficult part.

Participation takes time, particularly since the CDS initiative must work within the stakeholders' capacities and initiatives. Moving the CDS process too fast could undermine participation. Participation requires commitment building. It is a process that is based on ownership and partnership, and involves consultation, information sharing, debate, and empowerment. It is a fundamental ingredient of good local governance. Through participation, governments become more accountable, responsive, transparent, predictable, and effective in delivering services. A change in people's attitude and behavior is also necessary to sustain participation. Stakeholders must be initiated into the participatory process. Often, a project is designed without factoring in stakeholders' concerns. Stakeholders should be involved in all other phases of the CDS process, wherever appropriate.

The CDS is based on the belief that an adequate and timely mix of public, private and civil society initiatives can change the path of the city development. Given the uncertain environment, the cities must not lose focus of their targets and aim at the best possible utilization of limited financial and human resources. Moreover, with the high elasticity of capital flows in cities, the cities must show discipline and potential for growth.

The themes that are important in most CDS processes are:

i) Livelihood such as job creation, business development and sources of household income.
ii) Environmental sustainability and energy efficiency of the city and the quality of its service delivery.
iii) Spatial form and its infrastructure.
iv) Financial resources.
v) Governance.

The building blocks recommended for use in the CDS process include:

i) How to initiate the process.
ii) Establish the initial parameters and the scope of the CDS.
iii) Make a rapid assessment.
iv) Formulate your vision.
v) Identify your strengths-weaknesses-opportunities-threats (SWOT).
vi) Set your strategic thrusts.
vii) Build awareness.
viii) Start the implementation.

Cities without Slums (CWS) Programmes

The CWS programmes form an integral part of CDS considering that poverty reduction is an overriding objective that is reflected in the identification and development of key CDS sectors or themes. The CWS Action Plan was developed in July 1999 and launched by Nelson Mandela at the inaugural meeting of the CA in December.

In 2000 the CWS initiative was endorsed by the heads of state attending the UN Millennium Summit in September 2000. By 2020, it is to achieve a significant improvement in the lives of at least 100 million slum dwellers. The progress of this programme shall be evaluated upon the number of people who have gained an additional access to sanitation and secure tenure.

- Though the main purpose of the CWS initiatives is to eradicate slums by upgrading them, it also attempts to bring about better social, economic, environmental and governance conditions within poor urban communities. Thus the CWS initiative seeks to:

- Regularize security of tenure.
- Install and improve basic infrastructure, water supply, sanitation, SWM, access and circulation roads, storm water drainage and flood control, electricity supply, security lighting and public telephones.
- Removing or mitigating environmental hazards.
- Providing incentives for community management and maintenance.
- Constructing or rehabilitating community facilities including health centres, children's nurseries and public open space.
- Improving houses and relocating residents dislocated by the upgrading process with adequate compensation and assistance. However, resettlement must be minimized.
- Improving access to health care, education, and social support programmes to address issues such as security, violence, alcoholism and drug abuse.
- Enhancing livelihood opportunities by training and micro-credit for Small and Medium Scale Enterprises.
- Building more social infrastructure.

The CWS concentrates the poverty reduction programmes in each participating city on slums and squatter settlements where a majority of the urban poor live. While preparing the CWS, it is important to prepare a poverty map identifying the various slum and squatter settlements and comparing baseline, physical and socio-economic data for these areas with data for the entire city, to review the existing key physical and socio-economic characteristics that define citywide poverty, to estimate the relative poverty of each city and to compare it to the relative poverty in the slum areas, and to list all existing and proposed poverty reduction schemes. The costs of delivering shelter and providing basic services should be assessed.

According to Cities Alliance the principal indicators of CWS programme accomplishment are secure tenure and improved sanitation. It shall be based on resettling households from slums in danger areas, on strategic government reservations or private land otherwise and providing new, affordable serviced housing and sites in anticipation of future slum formation. However, the CWS looks beyond shelter provision and addresses other causes of poverty in the slums. It attempts to i) stimulate economic regeneration in order to create employment and income generation, ii) promote social development and improve systems of governance and empowerment in poor, urban communities, iii) link local infrastructure and services to wider strategic networks, and iv) assist in creating a more skilled and productive community through improved public health, education and welfare services.

The CWS Programme shall involve the following components:

i) Land Acquisition: This includes the subdivision and titling of land in existing slum settlements or for new low-cost housing and resettlement sites;

ii) On-Site/Off-Site Civil Works: This includes the up-gradation of public infrastructure and basic services and facilities. In some cases, it even involves reclamation.

iii) Provision of affordable serviced plots and housing.

iv) Finance and micro-finance to support house and plot purchase, small business enterprise and livelihood development, and home improvement loans.

v) Community training and capacity building programmes to empower and promote greater self-reliance and to support training for improved community organization, estate management and small business/livelihood activities.

vi) Institutional strengthening of key stakeholder groups includes training and capacity building of local government agencies, NGOs and micro-finance institutions.

vii) Education and awareness raising campaigns, including those directed to the private sector to encourage investment in pro-poor programs and in communities in relation to HIV, crime and drugs prevention, and the encouragement of community savings and loan programmes.

Being pro-poor is one of the features of the CDS that makes it superior to the CDP. The Johannesburg experience, however, suggests that pro-poor outcomes sometimes derive from factors outside the participatory process, such as a pro-poor legal framework. Even when every effort to include the poor in the participatory process is made, the balance of forces among stakeholders may mitigate against pro-poor outcomes. This may be as much the product of conflict between poor groups with different interests, as it is of elite capture of participatory processes. The poor may gain more from a boycott of the CDS participatory forum than by participating in it, when by implication they legitimate the process and its outcomes. Nevertheless, the poor can use participation as an effective device for influencing city scale strategic planning. However, how the poor participate in a CDS process should not be predetermined and must be appropriate for local political realities.

Conclusion

Urban poverty is complex, with varying dimensions. The policy-makers still have limited knowledge, not adequate perhaps for eradicating it. The enormity of the situation needs to be recognized before any comprehensive strategy can be formulated. The JNNURM seeks to address the issue of urban poverty in a limited, but a very positive way. While most cities envision themselves as slum-free by 2021, it is essential to understand that this will not necessarily hinder the rapidly spreading evils of poverty, because poverty is not purely concentrated in the slums. An appropriate strategy would entail better livelihood opportunities, job securities for those already employed, thus creating an environment of sustained welfare. Tenure security is something that deserves scads of attention. In this regard, the UPAIs of various countries in Asia were analyzed. A brief report of the Caplan UPAI is enclosed in Annexure XII. Strategies similar to those adopted in Caplan can be duplicated in India.

By incorporating such strategies, along with the basic services to the urban poor, and sallying the system-generated loopholes, India can create a programme that will benefit the poor, and provide for sustained development of each of the cities.

Bibliography

1. City Development Plans
   i. Ahmedabad
   ii. Vijaywada
   iii. Raipur
   iv. Rajkot
   v. Surat
   vi. Vishakhapatnam
   vii. Vadodara
   viii. Hyderabad
   ix. Kohima
   x. Chandigarh
   xi. Mysore
2. Supriti, Barnhardt; Sharon, M. and Ramanathan Ramesh (2002). *Urban Poverty Alleviation in India*, volume I & II: "Landmark Government Initiatives for the Urban Poor since Independence."
3. Various articles on www.indiatogether.com
4. "City Development Strategies to Reduce Poverty." Asian Development Bank, 2004.
5. www.citiesalliance.org

ANNEXURE-I

VADODARA

Overview

Vadodara has had a remarkably good strategy to assess the needs of the urban poor. It has studied these on the basis of surveys conducted by SEWA. It has also jotted down a list of services to be provided and the priorities attributed to each by the representatives of the urban poor. However, it does have certain flaws.

Demographic Aspect

Population: 13 lakh.

Projected Population: 17.54 lakh (in 2011), 14.69 lakh (in 2005).

Total Area of the City: 149 sq km.

No. of Slums: 336.

Slum Population: 2.57 lakh— 20% of the total population.

Projected Slum Population in 2005: 2.71 lakh.

No. of BPL Families: 96,000 (2.8 lakh people— 36% of the total population).

It can be noted that the percentage of the BPL population is larger than the percentage that lives in the slums. Also, all slum dwellers do not necessarily live below the poverty line. Hence it can be supposed that 16% of the population or more has not even been included in the surveys at all.

Analysis of the Existing Situation

According to Toolkit 2 of JNNURM, the existing infrastructure must be evaluated with reference to quality, quantity and coverage.

A. *Physical Infrastructure:* Vadodara's assessment of the quantity and coverage of physical infrastructure is exactly as per the JNNURM outline. The assessment has been done by VUDA (Vadodara Urban Development Authority). However, certain figures are missing, namely the length of state level roads in kms, an assessment of public transport and the total capacity of the buses.

As per quality, it finds mention in the CDPs as well. The CDP is quick to mention that the pressure of water supply is inadequate. This is because pipelines are extended as and when required from the nearest network. The problems related to the low quality of the sewerage system, storm water drainage, etc. are also adequately discussed.

On behalf of the VMC, the Gujarat Mahila Housing SEWA Trust carried out a slum survey in 297 slums in different parts of the city. It identified 5 basic services—water supply, sewerage, roads, SWM and street lighting. However, when it assessed that say, 96 slums have at least one of the 5 services, the question arises that they may not have considered the fact that some pockets of each of those 96 slums might not have even one of the above services, while others do. Hence, we would like to recommend that the figures should be quoted as "x% of households have at least one service" instead of "96 slums have at least one service".

Moreover, when SEWA stated that 11 slums have neither of the above services, an in-depth analysis of the standard and method of living of the dwellers in these slums should have been provided so as to provide a better understanding of the intricacies of slum life in order to provide these facilities and estimate how much they are needed. For example the CDP tells us that only 46% of the slums have drains. It is also important for the CDP to state that the 54% who don't have drains, divert their sewage into natural drains which pollutes the river, in order to provide a more realistic picture.

It is also noteworthy that the SEWA survey attended to 297 slums. There are 336 slums in Vadodara. Thus a question arises as to whether the needs of the other 39 slums were duly considered.

B. *Social Infrastructure*: According to the CDP, there are 4 hospitals run by the state government, 16 dispensaries, 3 mobile medical dispensaries, and 1 integrated health centre. In total, there are 827 health centres in Vadodara. The quality of health facilities cannot be too high, as the death rate has increased from 7.4% to 7.6%. There are

761 schools in Vadodara and 35% of them are Municipal Schools. What the CDP does not mention is the average fees of the non-Municipal Schools, and the number of students these schools cater to. The MS University however, has been given adequate coverage in this regard.

C. *Economic Base:* Occupational structure (2001): Agriculture–0.88%, Plantation workers–0.44, Manufacturing–0.88%, Trade, Commerce and Construction–97.80. Thus it can be seen that Vadodara is no agricultural economy and that it provides a large number of employment opportunities to migrants.

Participatory Approach in Analysis

It is truly commendable that the VMC has conducted two sets of opinion polls– one of a random sample of 5000 citizens of Vadodara and one of an equal sized sample of the urban poor. The latter sample involved NGOs working in slum areas participating in a day-long symposium organized by the United Way of Baroda. It may not be so that the NGOs adequately voiced the interests of the slum population and this can be seen in the fact that Social Infrastructure was ranked as the lowest priority when there are 500-700 cases of diarrhoea in the slum areas per year, along with a high incidence of malaria, cholera, jaundice and dysentery.

Vision and Strategies

Since 21% of the citizens of Vadodara and 18% of the urban poor ranked water supply as the highest priority, VMC plans to increase water supply coverage to 100% by 2011, construct additional priority works, reduce water losses, build capacity, increase water supply hours, etc. Sewerage and Solid Waste Management have been considered as next on VMC's list of priorities. Since Vadodara has suffered its share of floods (The urban poor, susceptible to the vagaries of nature have suffered even more) storm water drainage has been placed at third.

Remarkably, urban transportation and social infrastructure have featured as quite low on the priority scale. The latter cannot be ignored especially as the death rate has risen from

7.4 in 1981-1991 to 7.6 in 1991-2001, mainly due to inadequate health care. As per urban transportation, existing roads cover only 57% of the slums. Thus, 43% of the slums need better connectivity. Also, building toilets in 64% of the slums is essential.

The provision of housing has been given due importance in order to prevent the growth of slums and squatter settlements. The VMC has already constructed 3492 houses for the Economically Weaker Sections of Society and has taken up 392 more.

Recommendations

- Surveys should include 100% of the urban poor. The surveys done by both, SEWA and VMC do not take into account 16% of the population. These are below poverty line but do not live in slum areas.
- The length of state roads in kms, an assessment of public transport, and the total capacity of the buses must be mentioned.
- While noting the percentage of slums that have a particular service, figures must be mentioned in terms of percentage of slum households rather than percentage of slums as some pockets of each slum might not have that service while others do.
- It is also important to provide an in-depth analysis of how slums that don't have even one of the 5 basic services do without.
- Adequate data as per the number of students attending municipal and other schools, the average percentage of classes attended and an average of the fees of non-Municipal Schools must be provided.
- When it comes to vision and strategies, social infrastructure must be given higher importance, especially health infrastructure in the light of the high incidence of diarrhoea, cholera, jaundice and other diseases.
- Slums must be provided with better road connectivity.

ANNEXURE-II

AHMEDABAD

Overview

The CDP of Ahmedabad is a truly participatory one. The urban Poor have been allowed to decide whether they want to participate in this project or not. They contribute Rs. 2000 per household for physical development. If they are not able to do so, micro-credit facilities have been provided by SEWA.

Demographic Aspect

Population: 35.15 lakh (AMC area), 38.75 lakh (AUDA area)

Projected Population: Not provided

Total Area of the City: 4200 sq km (AUDA area)

No. of Slums: 710

Slum Population: 9.06 lakh-25.77% of the population

Projected Slum Population: Not provided

Population Below Poverty Line: 14.1% of the total population

It must be verified as to what percent of the BPL population lives in slums. That way, the part of the BPL population that doesn't, can be separately targeted for poverty alleviation programmes, as it is not likely to benefit by slum upgradation programmes under JNNURM.

Analysis of the Existing Situation

According to Toolkit 2 of JNNURM, the existing infrastructure must be evaluated with reference to quality, quantity and coverage. The CDP of Ahmedabad has provided a table on the quantity and coverage of basic facilities in the slums but its quality has not been evaluated. It is unclear as to how many hours water is supplied for, how frequent power cuts are, how often sewerage drains require maintenance, etc.

A. *Physical Infrastructure:* According to the CDP, only 3.5% of the slum households have private water connections, one-fifth of the slum population have access to private toilets, 61% have electricity and one-fifth have medical facilities. How those who don't have even one of these facilities live, requires an in-depth study. For example it is important to realize that those who don't have private toilets and are unable to queue for the community toilet (on an average 506 households queue for one public toilet according to the CDP) probably defecate in the open. Thus while more community or private toilets are being built, the diseases that might arise from open-air defecation must be identified by health camps and the people living in surrounding areas must be immunized. There are 10.5 lakh houses in Ahmedabad. 67% are used for residential purposes. The city has a large vacancy rate of 12.5% as the owners are wary of letting out their properties due to Rent Control. 66% of the slums are located upon private lands and 13% encroach upon government, and 17% on municipal land. 4% encroach upon lands held by other parties. There are only 710 slums housing over 9 lakh people.

B. *Social Infrastructure:* An analysis of the existing situation of social infrastructure has not been provided. However, NGOs have taken up the job of providing education and health facilities via informal educational programmes and those on maternal and child health. They have also undertaken income-generating programmes to improve the financial health of the slum dwellers.

C. *Economic Base:* Occupational structure (2001): The informal sector provides an income to 77% of Ahmedabad's work force according to a study done by Uma Rani and Ummi. The primary sector provides employment to 0.2% of the work force, the secondary to 3.09% and the tertiary to 96.71%.

Participatory Approach in Analysis

The CDP of Ahmedabad is one of the participatoriest with respect to the urban poor. Vadodara did special surveys by SEWA to evaluate the existing situation of the urban poor but it still had the poor represented by NGOs. Kohima did the same. Ahmedabad, however, allowed the urban poor to primarily decide whether to upgrade their homes and secondly contribute monetarily. Every HH that wishes to participate in the programme must pay Rs. 2000 for per unit physical development. For those that are unable to do so, micro-credit facilities shall be provided by SEWA. In all, the per unit cost of slum upgradation is estimated to be Rs. 15,800. The AMC shall contribute Rs. 11,500, the NGOs shall contribute Rs. 300, Industries and Social Institutions, Rs. 2000 and the Urban poor, Rs. 2000 for each HH.

However, the CDP of Ahmedabad has not provided any information on what stakeholders, especially those representing the urban poor, consider to be the most important to provide. A ranking of these services will help the AMC come up with a working schedule of the order to provide basic services in, if they can't do so simultaneously.

Vision and Strategies

The AMC has listed slums and *chawls* and geographically categorized them. Those plots that are necessary for providing infrastructural changes in the city have been excluded. The NGOs shall motivate the slum dwellers to participate in the project. They shall open a bank account and create a fund of theirs and the slum dwellers' contribution. The AMC shall then begin upgradation. Tenure security of 10 years has been granted to prevent the slum dwellers from being evicted as upgradation shall increase the rents.

As of December 2005, this project (called the Slum Networking Project) has been implemented in 41 slums. It has envisioned the provision of basic facilities— water supply, a sewerage network with individual toilets, street lighting, paved roads, and SWM, etc. The SNP also includes the mobilization of community savings groups, child and adult educational programmes, etc. The target cost of SNP is Rs. 10,000 lakhs.

The city is required to construct 60,000 houses for the urban poor. This will cost Rs. 750 crores. The youth training programme envisions providing vocational training to 20,000 young men and women. This shall cost Rs. 10 crores.

Recommendations

- It is important to provide an estimate of what the slum population shall be in the future so as to assess whether the services provided shall be sufficient or not. For example, if a community toilet is built to serve say, 10 people and the population grows to such that the same toilet ends up serving 20 people, it shall be more difficult to maintain, queues shall be longer than estimated and the problem of open-air defecation would not have been solved. Instead as we had already assessed that the slum population would double, we would have to construct another community toilet.
- The CDP should state the percentage of the BPL population that does not live in the slums. It should estimate where this part of the BPL population lives in order to ensure that it too, benefits from the poverty alleviation programmes.
- The quality of the existing infrastructure should be evaluated in order to assess future maintenance costs and what improvements are required.
- As mentioned above, an in-depth study of how those people who do not have a particular service do without because this often has implications upon the general environment of the slum.
- An analysis of the prevalent social infrastructure is necessary and cannot be ignored.

The AMC is currently tackling all problems arising due to a lack of BSUP simultaneously. In order to be more organized, it must, prioritize in consultation with the stakeholders and the data regarding BSUP.

ANNEXURE-III

RAJKOT

Overview

The CDP of Rajkot does not have a separate chapter on the urban poor hence the analysis of the existing infrastructural availability is not very detailed. However, Rajkot has a detailed and well worked out strategy for providing BSUP.

Demographic Aspect

Population: 1002000

Projected Population: 1484500 (in 2011)

Total Area of the City: 104.86 sq km

No. of Slums: 84 (notified)

Slum Population: 202371—13.63% of the total population

Projected Slum Population: Not provided

Population BPL: 147342 (14.7% of the city)

A statistics that could well be worth estimating is the percentage of the BPL population that does not live in the slums. It is important to identify where those that don't live in the notified slums live in order to ensure that they don't miss out on poverty alleviation programmes.

Analysis of the Existing Situation

A. *Physical Infrastructure:* The living condition of the urban poor has been evaluated by using types of roofs, types of floors, access to water and sanitation facilities as indicators. 59.62% of the slum population have tiled roofs, 74.52% have brick or PCC floors, 10% of the slum population do not have water but 34% have individual connections.

A study of whether the 10% of the population that do not get water bath in the drains or drink unpurified water is necessary to assess the health situation of the slums. 6% of slum households defecate in the open. 13% have individual toilets and 50% have an access to pay and use toilets. 90% of Rajkot have drains but the coverage of drainage and sewerage in slum areas is not clear.

B. *Social Infrastructure:* The Municipal Corporation runs 4 allopathic dispensaries and 1 Ayurvedic one. Each treats an average of 200 patients. There are three Mobile Dispensaries, which are run by NGOs with grants from the RMC. NGOs run 9 Family Welfare Centres. under the centrally sponsored Urban Malaria Scheme, melothyne powder has been sprayed into the gutters and fogging machines have been used to exterminate mosquitoes. Public awareness programmes have been organized.

C. *Economic Base:* The workforce in the slums is 32.46% of the slum population. 11.7% of these are unemployed, 18.04% are unskilled casual laborers, 5.4% are semi-skilled workers, and 3.5% are self-employed. 22% are industrial workers, 17.63% are casual workers, 9.44% are drivers and 8.25% are construction workers.

Participatory Approach in Analysis

The CDP has been prepared involving stakeholders through a 6-stage procedure. The authorities made appeals on Cable TV and newspapers, to call for greater participation. The city also aims at developing a participatory approach in delivery of services to the people, so as to bring about an improvement in the quality of their life. The urban poor have been indirectly represented.

Vision and Strategies

Firstly, the RMC intends to list all slum settlements, register all slum dwellers, and issue them identity cards prior to issuing tenure rights and starting improvement works. Next, all registered residents will be automatically eligible, to receive basic services like water, sanitation, electricity, health, etc. The RMC will decide the norms and standards of these services and how these will be delivered to the registered slum dwellers. Subsequent to this, after a particular amount of time decided upon by the RMC, those slum settlements that have attained the prescribed level of basic services shall be de-listed. Communities shall have an important role to play in the physical improvement and upgradation of the slums. The interests of women and children shall be kept in mind while improving the physical and socio-economic infrastructure available in the slums.

Under the JNNURM, Rajkot envisions zero slum areas, and a 100% access to BSUP. It plans to construct 500 houses, organize 14 slum network programmes, construct 50 km roads, and construct 25 pay and use toilets by the end of 2009. The RMC has an outlay of Rs.4820 lakhs for infrastructural improvements. It shall follow a pro-poor subsidization policy with full costs reflected on the budget of individual service providers. 20-25% of developed land shall be earmarked for EWS/LIG housing with a system of cross subsidization by December 2006.

Recommendations

- The percentage of BPL population that does not live in the notified slums must be estimated. In fact so should the percentage of LIG and EWS population. This is important so as to ensure that these groups that don't live in the slums don't miss out on poverty alleviation programmes.
- There are some areas that are not notified as slums but still have slum-like conditions. These should be classified as slums so that slum upgradation programmes benefit these.
- The infrastructural availability in the slums needs a more in-depth assessment. To get a better idea of the health situation, a study of how those sections of the slum population that are deprived of basic services live is essential.
- An estimate of the future slum population is worth studying in order to assess whether the infrastructure built under JNNURM shall be sufficient.
- Whether the social infrastructure can be accessed by slum dwellers must be analyzed.
- A prioritization of the basic services must be worked out in consultation with the stakeholders representing the urban poor.

ANNEXURE-IV

SURAT

Overview

Adequate emphasis has been made on the BSUP in the CDP prepared by Surat. The vision for Surat is to become a 'global city with global standards', by 2020. However, with the rapidly growing population, in order to sustain the current growth level, the city recognizes the need to strengthen the response mechanism of agencies to adequately address the growing demand.

Demographic Aspects

The CDP has taken care to carefully include details related to every aspect of the demographic component. The city at present has 312 slums, which constitute 19.24% of the city population, of which 80% are migrants. The growth rate of slums now stands at 1.46%, which is lower than that in the 1990s.The slums have encroached 64% of the total public land.

Economic Profile

Rapid growth of industrialization in the city and the scope of employment in trade and business has been responsible for the influx of migrants into the city, not only from rural Gujarat, but various other neighboring states. These migrants are the major inhabitants of the slums. Most of the slum population is involved in the informal sector.

Analysis of the Existing Situation

The CDP provides reasonably good detail of the existing situation with regard to the urban poor. While it is recognized that the existing situation with regard to the basic services is poor and dismal, efforts to bring about improvements in infrastructure are largely hampered owing to the continuously increasing number of slums. The situation in Surat as far as the urban poor is concerned seems to be better than the rest of the country, largely because of the improvement in services, after the plague epidemic of 1994. Almost 70% of the poor households have piped water supply.

The only detail missing from the CDP is with regard to the future projections of the housing requirements for the poor. The existing situation with regard to the housing and the future strategies have been explained well.

Vision and Strategies

The vision and strategies for Surat seem to be very sanguine. The CDP targets to provide piped water supply to the remaining 30% of the urban poor at an expense of Rs. 20 crore. The city also aims to take up a phased upgradation of infrastructure services and improved service delivery to the poor. The city wished to begin with a programme on slum relocation and rehabilitation, as a basis for plan two, that dreams of a city without slums.

Participatory Approach in Analysis

The city conducted a socio-economic & physical survey in the year 2005. Valuable inputs were received from the poor. The CDP suggests that the city is ready to bring about increased citizen's involvement in the development planning process, through active participation of voluntary organizations, citizen groups and NGOs.

Recommendations

The CDP for Surat is largely on the lines of the guidelines mentioned in toolkit 2. A positive aspect of the CDP is the degree of participation of people from all walks of life.

What is missing, however, is the analysis of the social infrastructure, particularly with regard to the urban poor. The CDP also needs to assess the future housing requirements of the slum population, so as to ensure that there is a match between demand and supply.

ANNEXURE-V

HYDERABAD

Overview

More than 33% of the total population of Hyderabad lives in slums and squatters. The growing contribution of the poor to the city's economy, and the lack of access to basic services, has prompted policies for infrastructure and social development.

Demographic Aspect

The CDP for Hyderabad provides a demographic analysis in good detail, for both the HUDA and the MCH administered areas. The analysis is complete with the current population scenario, future growth projections and population compositions. The analysis also includes details of the age structure and sex ratio.

As for details specific to the urban poor, the BPL population is estimated to be 540 thousand, of which 430 thousand live in the MCH areas, covering a total of 1142 slums. Hyderabad in all has 1631 slums. The slum population is heterogeneous, with Hindu, Muslim and Christian migrants settled there.

Economic Base

Most of the slum dwellers are migrants and depend on the informal sector for a livelihood. The contribution of the informal sector to the city economy is more than 30%.

Analysis of The Existing Situation

A separate chapter on the urban poor provides details related to both physical and social infrastructure.

A. *Physical Infrastructure:* The CDP provides a detail regarding the coverage of the infrastructural facilities to the poor. However, no details with regard to the quality of the services has been provided. While it is clear that services are not available to all the poor, how these services are availed has been left to the reader's imagination.

B. *Social Infrastructure:* Social Infrastructure has been dealt with in more detail. Schools and community halls are present in the slum areas. While considerable work has been done on estimating the literacy rates, no information is provided on the nature of these schools, i.e. whether primary or secondary; information with regard to the number of students enrolled or dropouts is also missing. With regard to health, 64 primary health centres have been set up, mostly in the MCH areas. The remaining slum areas lack health services.

Participatory Approach in Analysis

The participatory approach in Hyderabad involved two consultations with the stakeholders, which included the urban poor. These discussions facilitated identification of needs, their prioritization and preparation of an accepted development plan for the city focusing on the poor. These consultations are considered compulsory for the formulation of the master plan.

Vision and Strategies

The vision for Hyderabad is to become a 'World Class City'. The MCH is working at lowering the connection costs for water and easing the documentation procedure so as to ensure water supply to a larger number of the poor. As a part of the poverty reduction strategic plan, the city wishes to become slum free by 2021, provide basic services to the poor and bring about 100% literacy. The CDP provides pointers on the strategy that the city wishes to adopt. The city also plans to take up the slum networking program, for improving the drainage system in the city. It is believed that 40% of the tax revenues of the MCH will be devoted to improvement of facilities for the poor. Appropriate projections have been made so as to match demand with supply, as far as the housing requirements of the poor are concerned.

Recommendations

The CDP contains a number of headings, all of which, however, have not been dealt with in detail. It is important for the city to analyze the quality of the services available to the poor. A greater emphasis must be laid on the education and health services available to the poor. While the strategies lay a detailed emphasis on the provision of water to the poor, most other improvements have only been mentioned, without providing any strong strategy. The same should be covered. Moreover, since the participatory approach of Hyderabad is good, completing the above should not be a very difficult task.

ANNEXURE-VI

VIJAYAWADA

Overview

Vijayawada's Chapter V on the Basic Services to the Urban Poor is well written. The Key Challenges faced by the urban poor are very well evaluated. The Vijayawada CDP envisions the city without slums by 2021.

Demographic Aspect

Population: 1033562 (Vijayawada Urban Agglomeration Area)-2001, 8.45 lakh (VMC)-2001

Expected Future Population: 10.01 lakh (VMC-estimated in 2005), 11.77 lakh (VMC-projected in 2011)

Total Area of the City: 110.44 sq. km (VUA)

No. of Slums: Vijayawada–136, Mangalagiri–35

Slum Population: Vijayawada–263973–30.31% of the total population, Mangalagiri–30826–51.86% of the population

Projected Slum Population: Not provided

Percentage of BPL Population: 40% (2005-06)

Analysis of the Existing Situation

Vijayawada's CDP has an adequate coverage on the infrastructural services to the urban poor in terms of quantity and coverage. Quality, however, has not been specified.

A. *Physical Infrastructure:* The urban poor have an access to 110 lpcd of water supply, 2% access to sewerage, 35% coverage of storm water drains, 80% door-to-door garbage collection, no waste segregation, only 50% access to individual toilets but 75% access to community toilets. Only 20% of the slum population has an access to housing. There are no sewer lines in Mangalagiri.

   We would like to recommend that the VMC should provide an in-depth study of the quality of the existing infrastructure available to the urban poor—for how many hours is water supplied, how often do the storm water drains need repairing, etc. It is also important to provide an analysis of what the consequences of such a low access to sewerage are. For example, people may be diverting their waste water into natural drains which being untreated shall pollute the river water.

B. *Social Infrastructure:* There are 99 municipal schools in slum areas in Vijayawada, and 18 in Mangalagiri. However, data as to the number of students who attend these schools as a percentage of children aged 4 to 17 living in slum areas is lacking. There are 5 maternity hospitals and 17 urban health centres but gastroenteritis, malaria, diarrhoea, malnutrition and ringworm are common. The quality of these health centres needs to be evaluated and stressed upon.

C. *Economic Base:* Occupational structure (2001): The work-force constitutes only 30% of the population. Out of this the tertiary sector employs 71.81% (this has increased from 69.37% in 1991) and the secondary sector employs 21.64%. (which has dropped from 27.57% in 1991). The informal sector constitutes 30% of the total work-force. The incomes of the workers in this sector are 3-6 times lower than that of those in the organized sector.

Participatory Approach in Analysis

'Poverty and Slums' was a working group constituted to formulate the CDP. The Urban poor were represented by experts on urban poverty, CBOs and civil society organizations.

We believe that like Baroda, an NGO like SEWA should have been recruited to do a survey especially on the urban poor so as to evaluate their needs and interests. This would greatly solve the first of the key challenges outlined in the CDP the lack of authentic and dependable data. Also, the interests of the urban poor should have been evaluated in terms of priority to each basic service to be provided.

Vision and Strategies

Vijayawada envisions 100% literacy in the slums by 2020 by developing a 100% access to schooling, universal access to primary health facilities, adequate means of livelihood, tenurial security and affordable housing, relocation of slums, away from hazardous and vulnerable areas and provision of water, roads, sewerage, sanitation, clinics, schools, etc.

In collaboration with the State Government, which is keen on providing housing on a large scale under schemes like the Rajiv Gruhakalpa Scheme, the VMC plans to take up housing and tenure issues in a big way.

Under the JNNURM, VMC has requested an outlay of Rs. 533 crores for poverty alleviation, second in priority to storm water drainage. Its infrastructure restructuring strategy is clearly defined in tables and costs are estimated.

Recommendations

- An estimate of what the slum population shall be in 2011 is required in order to assess whether the infrastructure that shall be built under the JNNURM shall be sufficient to support it.
- The quality of existing physical and social infrastructure must be evaluated in order to provide a more realistic idea of how it can be improved.
- Like Vadodara, a reputed NGO must be recruited to do a survey on the conditions and needs of the urban poor, in order of priority. The vision and strategies to provide BSUP must be designed in line with the results of this survey.
- An in-depth analysis of how the urban poor survive in the households that don't have a particular facility, e.g. sewerage is important in the light of studying the consequences of a lack of the concerned facility.

ANNEXURE-VII

VISHAKHAPATNAM

Introduction

About 33% of the total urban population is living in slums, suggesting that urban poverty is a major issue in Vishakhapatnam. In view of the growing contribution of the poor to the city's economy, greater emphasis is being laid on analyzing the quality of their life and efforts to improve the same.

Demographic Aspect

The CDP gives a detailed analysis of the demographic aspect of the city, including projections for the future growth rate and the composition of population growth. The population is expected to be at 16.61 lakhs in 2011 and 20.99 lakhs in 2021. While the migration rate has come down, it is expected that the urban growth rate will continue to be high, largely because of the high natural growth rate.

Analysis of the Existing Situation

A. *Physical Infrastructure:* The CDP recognizes the prevalence of the urban poor, their lack of access to basic services, inadequate infrastructure and the issues with regard to vehicular pollution.

   While the numbers of slums have multiplied over the years, living conditions have not improved, suggesting additional pressure on the existing infrastructure. The poor spread out beyond slums in squatters and informal settlements are further subject to vagaries of the weather and insecurity. The addition of 32 slums inhabited by the poor has further added to the grimness of the situation. The women lead HH's in the slums are the poorest of the poor. While the infrastructure is known to be inadequate with regard to coverage, quality and quantity, a detailed analysis explaining each of these factors is missing. One can understand that the situation is largely due to the growing slum population, without a similar increase in the infrastructure.

'Population growth in Vizag is quite high and this would necessitate long-term planning and significant investments for improved service delivery.'

However, no substantial explanation is provided for the absence in infrastructural growth.

The existing situation with regard to housing has been dealt with in a better manner. It is recognized that the existing housing is small, congested and unsanitary, and that there is a need to construct pucca houses, with minimal financial contributions from the beneficiaries. This aspect has been explained. Issues relating to water availability and coverage have not been dealt with in detail.

B. *Social Infrastructure:* Data related to literacy levels is missing in the CDP. The number of schools and health centres serving the poor has not received adequate mention. While there are 15 urban primary health centres, details regarding the extent of their coverage is missing.

C. *Economic Base:* The growth of industries in Vizag over the past decade and the port has made available a large number of employment opportunities to the people. There has been a large-scale influx of migrants from neighboring areas, mostly the poor, who are working with the informal sector.

Vision and Strategies

'The vision of Vizag is to become a city without slums by 2021'. In order to achieve these goals, the GVMC has clearly outlined a set of integrated slum development programs, covering all aspects of the slum including basic services, literacy, health and livelihood. Priority has clearly been given to the need for housing, in consultation with the beneficiaries. The GVMC seeks to strengthen community-based organizations, in line with the participatory approach to target social infrastructure needs.

Recommendations

While the CDP is clear on what the future strategies ought to be, including tables of quantities and expenditures, the portion on the existing situation has not been dealt with in a detailed manner. In order to be able to understand the link between Demand & Supply, details of the existing situation must be presented in an elaborate manner. The CDP has stark semblance with that of Hyderabad.

ANNEXURE-VIII

KOHIMA

Overview

The CDP of Kohima is inclusive in every way. Providing basic services to the urban poor has been especially emphasized upon while enumerating KMC's vision and strategies. The baseline data on the existing situation has been presented in adequate detail and supplemented by a socio-economic survey conducted for 1000 HHs in the Kohima Planning Area as a part of the ADB funded North Eastern Region Urban Development Project (NERUDP).

Demographic Aspect

Population: 115283 (in GKPA-Greater Kohima Planning Area), 77030 (KMC-Kohima Municipal Council Area)

Projected Population in GKPA: 147,382 (in 2011); 129,470 (in 2005)

Total Area of the City: 63.55 sq km

No. of Slums: 6 localities notified as slums

Slum Population: 20194 (26.2% of the total city population, 17.3% of the GKPA population)

Projected Slum Population: Not provided

No. of BPL Families: 1347 (6384 people–23.7% of the total population)

About 34.9% of the total BPL population lives in the slums. Hence, the slum upgradation programmes shall not affect 65.1% of the BPL population. Though as the CDP mentions, there are no squatter settlements in Kohima, the 65.1% of the BPL population that are not living in the notified slum areas must be living somewhere. Details as to where and how this 65.1% of the BPL population lives is essential to ensure that they too benefit from the JNNURM.

Analysis of the Existing Situation

The CDP of Kohima provides a matrix, enumerating in detail, a profile of each slum with respect to location, population, housing type and infrastructure. It has kept the JNNURM Toolkit requirements of a report of quality, quantity and coverage of infrastructure in mind.

A. *Physical Infrastructure:* All six notified slums have been listed. Kitsubozou or Chota Basti is the oldest settlement in Kohima. 70% of the habitants live in their own houses–usually 'kutcha' bamboo structures, 40% have tap water, 73% have septic tanks with toilets but 50% of the households discharge their sewerage directly into drainage channels, 32% have lined drains while 68% have opened unlined drains. This area is vulnerable to landslides.

   The main problem faced in New Market is that drains are choked. This is because most of the slum dwellers run slaughterhouses and due to lack of waste disposal, dump their waste into the drains. 35% of the housing is rented. Details about tenure security, however, have not been provided in the CDP.

   A map has been provided to explain the housing status in Kohima. Since more than 95% of the Naga population is classified as ST, land ownership is mostly private. Most of the residents own land under Article 371 of the Constitution. Those who live in a rented accommodation are primarily migrants from other states.

   What is commendable about the infrastructure table of the BSUP section of the CDP of Kohima is that it provides complete details about the lack of infrastructure, and its consequences (eg. because drains are mostly open and unlined, there is a high incidence of cholera and hepatitis).

B. *Social Infrastructure:* No details pertaining to Social Infrastructure are provided. Though there are departments for primary health and primary education in the Kohima's institutional set-up, their activities have not been specified in the Analysis of the Existing Situation.

C. *Economic Base:* The labour force consists of 41.3% of the population, 54.5% of the sample population is engaged in various government sector jobs, 17.5% are self-employed. They own their own shops and businesses.

Only 5.7% is engaged in agriculture, 1.2% in traditional crafts, 2.5% in manufacturing, and 18.6% in other activities. Only 0.3% of the sample population was unemployed.

Participatory Approach in Analysis

The urban poor were duly represented in the stakeholder consultations by the primary stakeholders–NGOs, CBOs, Women's Self Help Groups, etc. They were also represented by their elected representatives and government officials, who served as secondary stakeholders. The basis for prioritization of issues has been provided in full detail. The stakeholders were asked to rank their priorities and results were tabulated. The highest priority is to be provided to drainage followed by water supply, precautionary measures to reduce damage due to landslides, SWM, transportation and sewerage in that order.

We would like to recommend that sewerage should be treated with due importance. Untreated waste water being diverted into streams, etc. pollutes river water. There is only one sewerage drain in Kohima's slum areas and open defecation is a major health issue causing various health problems.

Vision and Strategies

Kohima's CDP envisions a better "access to housing and basic infrastructure" for the urban poor. So far, the coverage of poverty alleviation plans since 1989 has been inadequate. According to the CDP, only 9% of the BPL population has been benefited. However, the basis for arriving at this figure is unclear. Building footpaths, public wells, sewerage drains, roadside drains, public toilets and roads shall do this. The total outlay for slum upgradation is Rs.56.31 million. However, the investment needed is Rs.258.315 million. Thus this must be clarified.

Recommendations

- An estimate of the projected slum and BPL population in 2011 must be provided in order to assess whether the infrastructure developed under JNNURM shall serve a large proportion of the urban poor.

- Details must be provided as to how the 65.1% of the BPL population, which does not live in the slums, live. As the CDP states, some high-income groups also stay in the slums while majority of the BPL population lives in areas that are not notified as slums. For the JNNURM to really serve the urban poor, this is essential.
- An assessment of the quality, quantity and coverage of Social infrastructure must be provided in order to provide a better idea of the living standards of the urban poor and to find remedies to the chronic health problems in the slums.
- The CDP should provide the basis for arriving upon the fact that only 9% of the BPL population is benefited by the past poverty alleviation programmes. An in-depth study of why this is true is also required.

Finally, the amount of investment required for slum upgradation must be clarified.

ANNEXURE-IX

RAIPUR

Demographic Aspect

The demographic aspect has been dealt with in reasonable detail. The current slum population is estimated to be 3,68,956, covering over 192 slums, in an area of about 300 hectares. The population projections suggest a population of 15 lacs for Raipur by the year 2011. The components for population increase include population explosion, and immigration. The latter being the main cause for the growth of slums.

Analysis of the Existing Situation

The analysis of the existing situation with regard to the urban poor are missing in the CDP. While it has been recognized that the slums have unhealthy living conditions and sources of pollution for social and environmental status of the town, no details to substantiate it have been provided.

As for the economic base, a majority of the people is working in the informal sector.

The authorities have clarified that financial and natural constraints are not binding for the growth of infrastructure, while the administrative and technical constraints are being removed in a phased manner suggesting that the infrastructure growth should be fast, and would benefit the poor.

Vision and Strategies

The only vision with regard to slums and the urban poor is a slum upgradation programme that the city wishes to take up as a part of the JNNURM. The cost for the same has been estimated at Rs. 232 crore. The same has priority after road development in the city.

The CDP talks about promoting the informal sector, which is a source of livelihood to the urban poor, more so since it has become evident that the informal sector complements the formal sector.

Participatory Approach in Analysis

No details mentioning the participation of the urban poor either directly or indirectly in the preparation of the CDP have been provided. The CDP contains a mention of the field visits to be completed by the authorities in the future. However, no details of the same have been provided.

Recommendations

We would recommend a primary level survey of the urban poor, to be able to understand the quality and coverage of services available to them. While the slums have been easily tagged as unhealthy for the city environment, no concrete policies for improvement have been provided. It is essential that the same be taken up. This would be in line with the recommendations made under the Toolkit 2.

ANNEXURE-X

CHANDIGARH

Overview

Chandigarh has provided no information on the status of the urban poor except a brief description in which the subject has been dealt with in an extremely cursory fashion.

Demographic Aspect

Chandigarh has a population of 9.01 lakh and it expects it to rise to 13.38 lakh in 2011. The city covers an area of 150 sq km. Details about the number of slums, the number of slum dwellers as a percentage of the total population and the percentage of people living BPL have not been mentioned.

Analysis of the Existing Situation

According to Toolkit 2 of JNNURM, the existing infrastructure must be evaluated with reference to quality, quantity and coverage. Infrastructural details have been provided but its coverage in slum areas has not been discussed. ... mentions that 155 of households are living in unauthorized tenements or temporary structures but even these enjoy a 100% access to basic services, namely water supply, sanitation, primary education, and primary health.

Participatory Approach in Analysis

The CDP is unclear on how well the interests of the urban poor were represented while the CDP was being formulated.

Vision and Strategies

The internal earmarking of the budget has been provided for a period of 7 years. Otherwise the vision and strategy for providing BSUP is unclear.

Recommendations

A separate chapter must be dedicated to BSUP. It should contain the demographics of the slum population, the BPL population, how much of the BPL population lives in slums, and the projected slum and BPL population. A thorough survey must be done of the services that exist in the slum areas and an in-depth study should be done of those households who do not have even one of these services. A step-by-step strategy for providing BSUP should be spelled out. The way these services should be prioritized should depend upon those stakeholders that represent the urban poor.

ANNEXURE-XI

S.No.	City	Emphasis on Urban Poor	Other Details
1.	Ahmedabad	Whether the CDP has been participatory with respect to the urban poor	Indirectly represented by NGOs
		Emphasis	Separate chapter on urban poor and housing given
		Population/Households	Slum Population– 9 lakhs No. of Slum Households– 1.76 lakh– 1/4th population of AMC and 1/5th of AUDA
		Access to basic services	Details given, deficient in terms of basic services. Zero open defecation envisioned
2.	Surat	Whether the CDP has been participatory with respect to the urban poor	Indirectly represented by NGOs
		Emphasis	Separate Chapter on Housing and slums. Map provided
		Population/Households	Slum Population– 5.69 lakhs No. of Slums– 312 No. of Slum Households– 93655– 19% of total population
		Access to basic services	Discussed, given in table. 72% of households have private water taps and 35% have private toilets. City without slums envisioned
3.	Vadodara	Whether the CDP has been participatory with respect to the urban poor	Indirectly represented by NGOs who participated in an opinion poll ranking the basic services in order of priority. Special survey on the existing situation of the urban poor done by SEWA
		Emphasis	Status well examined. Details provided. Separate section on 'Urban Poor' included in the CDP
		Population/Households	No. of Slums– 336; No. of Slum Households– 51439 (20% of total population)
		Access to basic services	80% have access to water, 46% to drainage, 42% to toilets. 190 slums identified for providing on-site services

S.No.	City	Emphasis on Urban Poor	Other Details
4.	Rajkot	Whether the CDP has been participatory with respect to the urban poor	Indirectly represented in 4 group meetings by RMC
		Emphasis	Status well presented and map provided
		Population/Households	84 notified slums as per 2001 20% of RMC resides in slums
		Access to basic services	10% has no access to water, 6% defecates in the open. Slum improvement dealt separately indicating projects to be undertaken with criteria of creating zero slum area and access to all
5.	Vishakha-patnam	Whether the CDP has been participatory with respect to the Urban Poor	Represented in stakeholder consultations
		Emphasis	Status presented elaborately
		Population/Households	No. of Slums– 472 in GVMC, 41% of total population as per 2005 data, 24% as per 2001
		Access to basic services	60% of slum area has drinking water, 25% has sewerage. Strategies to attain achievable goals formulated by city without slums envisioned by 2021
6.	Vijaywada	Whether the CDP has been participatory with respect to the Urban Poor	
		Emphasis	Well provided. Information of poverty reduction initiatives and schemes also discussed
		Population/Households	30% of slum population in municipal areas, 52% in peripheral areas
		Access to basic services	20% of slums have water supply, 2% have sewerage and 75% have access to community toilets. Comprehensive plan for urban poor given
7.	Raipur	Whether the CDP has been participatory with respect to the Urban Poor	Stakeholder consultations not taken. The CDP completely misses the views and opinions of the people

S.No.	City	Emphasis on Urban Poor	Other Details
		Emphasis	The section on urban poor provides only a list of the slums. Details not provided
		Population/Households	Not provided
		Access to basic services	Not provided. Vision presented in a generalized manner. Specific details on strategies are not provided
8.	Hyderabad	Whether the CDP has been participatory with respect to the urban poor	Broad based stakeholder consultations held. Indirectly represented
		Emphasis	Separate chapter on basic services to urban poor provided
		Population/Households	14% of population BPL, 39% lives in the slums
		Access to basic services	Details given. Basic infrastructure in slums-minimal and inadequate. Separate plan for urban poor envisioned
9.	Kohima	Whether the CDP has been participatory with respect to the urban poor	The urban poor are secondary stakeholders. Indirectly represented by NGOs
		Emphasis	Chapter 6 of the CDP gives a profile of the urban poor
		Population/Households	24% of the city identified as BPL, 26% lives in slums
		Access to basic services	9% benefited through anti-poverty programmes. 25% have individual toilets, access to PHED water supply is absent, poor education levels
10.	Chandigarh	Whether the CDP has been participatory with respect to the urban poor	
		Emphasis	... has been dedicated to the basic services for urban poor. Details have not been provided
		Population/Households	15% of population living in unauthorized or temporary structures
		Access to basic services	100% access to water, sanitation, education and health

ANNEXURE-XII

International Poverty Alleviation Programs

Caplan

The city of Caplan is the capital of the island province of Oriental Mindoro, 130 km south of Manila. As of 2000 the HH poverty ratio in the city was 33.7%. One of the major dimensions of poverty in the city of Caplan has been income poverty. This has translated into health and education poverty, owing to the lack of resources to avail health and education facilities.

About 26.96% of the population at present lives in informal settlements, thus suggesting that there is also a problem of housing and tenure security. Combating poverty is one of the major thrusts of the city government.

To deal with income and employment related issues of poverty, the government allowed a large number of investors to invest in the city. Moreover, various efforts were made to encourage domestic tourism. The emergence of international chains of fast food joints, shopping malls and resorts provided employment opportunities to a large number of people. To address the issues of livelihood, the government also introduced micro-finance schemes for the youth, women and the old; enabling them to set up individual units for livelihood generation.

To address health and poverty, the government initiated a health insurance scheme, wherein the government paid the insurance premium for those who were registered in the program. The program was an effective and successful program against health and poverty.

As for education, the city government keeps a large portion of its annual budget for the maintenance and upgradation of public schools. This, keeping in view of the belief that the poor send their children to public schools. The city has also introduced the city college scholarship scheme, available to 500 students from poor families who wish to pursue higher studies.

In order to provide land tenure security to the poor, the government has initiated a number of schemes, one of which is the City Mortgage Program, wherein a National Home Mortgage Finance Company purchases the land occupied by the informal settlers from its actual owner. The poor, through a village community that they have set up, pay the corporation for the amortization for the property.

Reference

1. The Cities Alliance, located at Washington D.C., is a global coalition of cities and their development partners committed to scaling up successful approaches to poverty reduction.

Poverty Alleviation in Rural India – Strategy and Programmes*

6

At the beginning of the new millennium, 260 million people in the country did not have incomes to access a consumption basket which defines the poverty line. Of these, 75 per cent were in the rural areas. India is home to 22 per cent of the world's poor. Such a high incidence of poverty is a matter of concern in view of the fact that poverty eradication has been one of the major objectives of the development planning process. Indeed, poverty is a global issue. Its eradication is considered integral to humanity's quest for sustainable development. Reduction of poverty in India, is, therefore, vital for the attainment of international goals.

Agricultural wage earners, small and marginal farmers and casual workers engaged in non-agricultural activities, constitute the bulk of the rural poor. Small land holdings and their low productivity are the cause of poverty among households dependent on land-based activities for their livelihood. Poor educational base and lack of other vocational skills also perpetuate poverty. Due to the poor physical and social capital base, a large proportion of the people are forced to seek employment in vocations with extremely low levels of productivity and wages. The creation of employment opportunities for the unskilled workforce has been a major challenge for development planners and administrators.

Poverty alleviation has been one of the guiding principles of the planning process in India. The role of economic growth

* *Courtesy*: Planning Commission, Tenth Five-Year Plan

in providing more employment avenues to the population has been clearly recognised. The growth-oriented approach has been reinforced by focusing on specific sectors which provide greater opportunities to the people to participate in the growth process. The various dimensions of poverty relating to health, education and other basic services have been progressively internalised in the planning process. Central and state governments have considerably enhanced allocations for the provision of education, health, sanitation and other facilities which promote capacity-building and well-being of the poor. Investments in agriculture, area development programmes and afforestation provide avenues for employment and income. Special programmes have been taken up for the welfare of scheduled castes (SCs) and scheduled tribes (STs), the disabled and other vulnerable groups. Anti-poverty programmes that seek to transfer assets and skills to people for self-employment, coupled with public works programmes that enable people to cope with transient poverty, are the third strand of the larger anti-poverty strategy. The targetted public distribution system (TPDS) protects the poor from the adverse effects of a rise in prices and ensures food and nutrition security at affordable prices.

The success of the anti-poverty strategy can be gauged from the decline in poverty levels from 37.27 per cent in 1993-94 to 27.09 per cent in 1999-2000 in the rural areas. In absolute terms, the number of rural poor fell below the 200 million mark for the first time since 1973-74. However, this achievement falls short of the Ninth Plan projections. At the beginning of the Plan, it was projected that, with a growth target of 6.5 per cent per annum during the Plan period, only 18.61 per cent of the population would be below the poverty line by 2001.

This shortfall can be attributed largely to the uneven performance of states in poverty alleviation. The distribution of poor across states is also disparate, with Uttar Pradesh, Bihar, Madhya Pradesh, West Bengal and Orissa accounting for 69 per cent of the poor in 1999-2000. Figure 6.1 depicts broad estimation of rural poverty across major states between 1993-94 and 1999-2000.

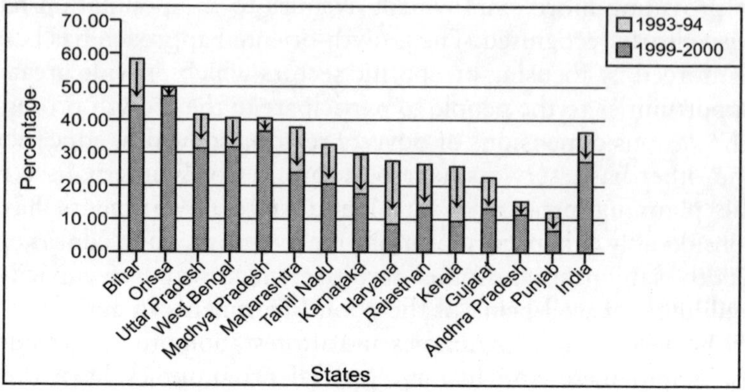

Fig. 6.1: Incidence of Rural Poverty in India

Kerala, Haryana, Bihar, Himachal Pradesh, Karnataka and Rajasthan experienced a sharp reduction in poverty levels (a drop of more than 12 percentage points between 1993-94 and 1999-2000). Uttar Pradesh, West Bengal and Tamil Nadu also registered significant reduction in poverty (8-12 percentage points). However, Orissa and Madhya Pradesh have shown virtually no reduction in poverty levels. In fact, these are the states where the absolute number of poor has actually gone up between 1993-94 and 1999-2000.

Anti-Poverty Programmes in the Ninth Plan

Integrated Rural Development Programme/Swarnajayanti Gram Swarozgar Yojana

The Integrated Rural Development Programme (IRDP), introduced in selected blocks in 1978-79 and universalised from 2 October 1980 has provided assistance to rural poor in the form of subsidy and bank credit for productive employment opportunities through successive plan periods. Subsequently, Training of Rural Youth for Self Employment (TRYSEM), Development of Women and Children in Rural Areas (DWCRA), Supply of Improved Tool Kits to Rural Artisans (SITRA) and Ganga Kalyan Yojana (GKY) were introduced as sub-programmes of IRDP to take care of the specific needs of the rural population. These schemes were, however, implemented as 'stand alone programmes', an approach which substantially detracted from their effectiveness. The Mid-Term Appraisal of the Ninth Plan had indicated that these sub-programmes "presented a matrix of multiple programmes without desired linkages". The programme suffered from sub critical investments, lack of bank credit, over-crowding in certain projects, and lack of market linkages. The programme was basically subsidy-driven and ignored the processes of social intermediation necessary for the success of self-employment programmes. A one-time provision of credit without follow-up action and lack of a continuing relationship between borrowers and lenders also undermined the programme's objectives.

The marginal impact of self-employment programmes led to the constitution of a committee by the Planning Commission in 1997 to review self-employment and wage-employment programmes. The committee recommended the merger of all self-employment programmes for the rural poor and a shift from the individual beneficiary approach to a group-based approach. It emphasised the identification of activity clusters in specific areas and strong training and marketing linkages. The committee's recommendations were accepted by the Government.

On April 1, 1999, the IRDP and allied programmes, including the Million Wells Scheme (MWS), were merged into a single programme known as Swarnajayanti Gram Swarozgar Yojana (SGSY). The SGSY is conceived as a holistic programme of micro-enterprise development in rural areas with emphasis on organising the rural poor into self-help groups, capacity-building, planning of activity clusters, infrastructure support, technology, credit and marketing linkages. It seeks to promote a network of agencies, namely the District Rural Development Agencies (DRDAs), line departments of state governments, banks, NGOs and Panchayati Raj Institutions (PRIs) for implementation of the programme. The SGSY recognises the need to focus on key activities and the importance of activity clusters. The programme has in-built safeguards for the weaker sections. It insists that 50 per cent of the self-help groups must be formed exclusively by women and that 50 per cent of the benefits should flow to SCs and STs. There is also a provision for disabled beneficiaries. The programme is credit-driven and subsidy is back-ended. The credit and subsidy ratio is pegged at 3:1. The subsidy is fixed at 30 per cent of the project cost subject to a maximum of Rs. 7,500 per individual beneficiary for those in the general category and 50 per cent of the project cost subject to a maximum of Rs. 10,000 in the case of SCs/STs. In the case of group projects, the subsidy is 50 per cent of the project cost subject to a ceiling of Rs. 1.25 lakh. Funds under the scheme are shared between the centre and state governments in the ratio of 75:25. The new approach to self-employment has made significant contribution to the empowerment of beneficiaries as evidence from the evaluation of SGSY in Tamil Nadu shows (Box 6.1).

Box: 6.1

Self-Help Groups under Swarnjayanti Gram Swarozgar Yojana (SGSY) in Tamil Nadu

I. In Mathur village of the Dharmapuri district of Tamil Nadu, 100 women from eight self-help groups were trained in fruit processing by a non-government organisation (NGO). They availed of assistance under SGSY to run a fruit processing unit registered under the name of Sathyamurthi Mahalir Mandram in May 2000. In addition, the unit was provided Rs. 8 lakh under the SGSY infrastructure fund for purchasing pouching, shrink pack and other machines. The unit produces fruit squash, jam, ready-to-serve beverages, pickle, etc. made from mango, pineapple, grape, lemon and onion under the brand name of SWARNA. It has been granted a Fruit Products Order (FPO) licence. The unit has engaged the services of a food technologist and emphasis is laid on the quality of the products, proper hygiene and attractive packaging. SWARNA products are sold to local retail shops and in district and state-level exhibitions. The marketing of SWARNA products is done by two NGOs — Sarvodaya Sangam, Vellore and Sarvodaya Sangam, Thirupatthur. The group members maintain accounts themselves.

Members of the group engaged in processing activities are given employment on rotation basis and the monthly income of a member is not less than Rs. 1,000. As a result of the high volume of sales, the group has been able to construct a new building for housing unit at a cost of Rs. 10 lakh. Apart from raising the economic status of the group members, this venture has made the members more aware and they are actively involved in Government schemes, camps and campaigns. They attend gram sabha meetings and have made representations for provision of basic facilities in their village and overall development of the area.

II. In the Vilpatti village of Dindigul district, 45 below poverty line women from three self-help groups assisted by an NGO and aided under SGSY received training in dry flower arrangement from an art gallery. In November 2000, under the cluster approach, the three groups formed a confederation named BIRIJA and are engaged in the collecting, processing and selling dry flowers. BIRIJA has a marketing tie-up with an art gallery to conduct exhibitions and sell their finished products. Within six months of the commencement of this venture, monthly sales touched to Rs. 70,000. The members receive an average net income of Rs. 1500 per month. Apart from improving their living conditions, the members have gained confidence and are actively involved in social work, participating in the movement against illicit arrack and in gram sabha meetings.

Source: Ministry of Rural Development, Government of India.

Implementation of the programme between 1999-2000 and 2001-02 has highlighted many areas of concern. While the IRDP concentrated on individual beneficiaries, the SGSY laid greater emphasis on social mobilisation and group formation. However, the DRDAs, responsible for administering the programme, did not have the requisite skills in social mobilisation. Linkages with NGOs, which could have facilitated this process, were also not in place. The programme, therefore, suffered in the initial years. Information on the physical and financial performance of IRDP/SGSY during the Eighth and Ninth Plans is given at Annexure-6.1. Central releases were substantially lower than the allocation as the field offices were not in a position to organise self-help groups which could be provided financial assistance. Credit mobilisation also suffered in the process. Against a target of Rs. 9,611 crore of credit, the achievement during the last three years has been only Rs. 3,235 crore, i.e. 33.66 per cent of the target. In the last three years of the Ninth Plan, 7,67,141 self-help groups were formed. While 9,34,000 individuals were assisted in 1999-2000, 10,30,000 individuals were provided support in 2000-01. The coverage was considerably lower than around 2.2 million beneficiaries under IRDP every year during the Eighth Plan period.

Wage Employment Programmes

Wage employment programmes, an important component of the anti-poverty strategy, have sought to achieve multiple objectives. They not only provide employment opportunities during lean agricultural seasons but also in times of floods, droughts and other natural calamities. They create rural infrastructure which supports further economic activity. These programmes also put an upward pressure on market wage rates by attracting people to public works programmes, thereby reducing labour supply and pushing up demand for labour. While public works programmes to provide employment in times of distress have a long history, major thrust to wage employment programmes in the country was provided only after the attainment of self-sufficiency in foodgrains in the 1970s. The National Rural Employment Programme (NREP) and Rural Landless Employment Guarantee Programmes (RLEGP) were started in the Sixth and Seventh Plans.

Jawahar Rozgar Yojana/Jawahar Gram Samridhi Yojana

The NREP and RLEGP were merged in April 1989 under the Jawahar Rozgar Yojana (JRY). The JRY was meant to generate meaningful employment opportunities for the unemployed and underemployed in rural areas through the creation of economic infrastructure and community and social assets. Initially, the JRY also included the Indira Awas Yojana (IAY) and the MWS. Both these schemes were made into independent schemes in 1996. Under JRY, 73,764.83 lakh mandays of employment were generated till 1998-99. Employment generation progressively declined over the years, partly due to lower central allocations in the Ninth Plan and partly due to the increasing cost of creating employment.

A major proportion of JRY funds was spent on roads and buildings. Over 47 per cent of the employment generated benefited SCs/STs. The share of landless labourers among the beneficiaries was 36 per cent. The village community found the assets created under the programme useful. However, against 40 per cent of population in a village panchayat who sought work, only 15 per cent were actually employed.

The JRY was revamped from 1 April 1999 as the Jawahar Gram Samridhi Yojana (JGSY). It now became a programme for the creation of rural economic infrastructure with employment generation as a secondary objective. The 60:40 wage labour/material ratio in the JRY was relaxed. The programme is implemented by the village panchayats and provides for specific benefits to SCs/STs, the disabled and the maintenance of community assets created in the past. Since inception it has generated 27 crore mandays of employment each year (on an average), a substantial drop from the 103 crore mandays generated under JRY in the year 1993-94.

The works taken up under JGSY have not been comprehensively evaluated for their quality and employment potential. Initial reports from the states, however, indicate that since every village panchayat has to be covered by the scheme, many panchayats get less than Rs. 10,000 per annum. Except for states like Kerala, West Bengal and Orissa, where village panchayats cover large areas and get substantial funds under the scheme, in other states most panchayats get less than Rs. 50,000 per annum. Benefits to the SCs/STs and the disabled have to be earmarked. In addition, the administrative expenses of the panchayat and expenditure on assets already created are to be met from JGSY funds. In effect, panchayats are left with very little money to take up meaningful infrastructure projects.

Employment Assurance Scheme

The Employment Assurance Scheme (EAS) was launched on 2 October 1993 covering 1,778 drought-prone, desert, tribal and hill area blocks. It was later extended to all the blocks in 1997-98. The EAS was designed to provide employment in the form of manual work in the lean agricultural season. The works taken up under the programme were expected to lead to the creation of durable economic and social infrastructure and address the felt-needs of the people. The scheme prohibited construction of buildings for religious purposes, monuments, memorials, welcome gates, panchayat buildings, government office buildings and buildings for higher secondary schools and colleges. It also provided for maintenance of assets created in the past under the scheme. Initially, the scheme was demand-driven but from 1999, resources were allocated to states based on the incidence of poverty.

The EAS is a centrally-sponsored scheme, with the Centre providing 75 per cent of the funds and the states 25 per cent. The zila parishads and panchayat samitis were the implementing agencies. Annexure 6.1 provides details of the physical and financial performance of the scheme during the Eighth and Ninth Plan periods. While 10,719.59 lakh mandays of employment were generated during the Eighth Plan, 4,717.74 lakh mandays of employment were generated in the first year of the Ninth Plan. Employment generation went down in subsequent years. The allocations between 1999-2000 and 2001-02 were also lower than the first two years of the Ninth Plan because watershed projects taken up for implementation under the EAS before April 1999 were transferred to Integrated Wasteland Development Programme (IWDP).

Though the creation of community assets has important spin offs for rural poverty and development, the impact of these programmes on employment and income has been limited. The universalisation of the scheme severely eroded its basic objective of providing assured employment in areas of extreme poverty and chronic unemployment. Allocations were based on a fixed criterion that did not specifically provide for regionally differentiated needs. This led to a very thin spread of resources across the country. As a result, even in the poorer regions, employment was provided for only 31 days (Programme Evaluation Organisation Study-2001). In many states, the works taken up were not labour-intensive. Cases of bogus reporting and fudged muster rolls have been reported. The efficacy of the programme was also affected by faulty project selection and the absence of a coherent plan which integrated EAS projects in a long-term development strategy.

In spite of their many shortcomings, wage employment schemes have proved beneficial in some respects. They created much-needed rural infrastructure. The programmes are self-targeting in nature since only the poor come to work at minimum wage rates. The various works undertaken created demand for unskilled labour and exerted upward pressure on wage rates. The programmes have played a major role in protecting consumption patterns of the rural poor during natural calamities. A study conducted in four drought-affected districts of Rajasthan found that the consumption of foodgrains was higher in the drought years compared to normal years due to the wage employment programmes. Since PRIs were associated with the implementation of JRY/JGSY and EAS, government financing of panchayats strengthened these institutions and promoted better coordination between the village community and government departments. Box 6.2 summarises the findings of evaluation studies of EAS/JRY conducted in Rajasthan and Uttar Pradesh.

Box: 6.2

Impact of Rural Infrastructure/Wage Employment Programmes

A study conducted in Ajmer, Udaipur, Pali and Jaisalmer in Rajasthan for the period 1995-2001 observed that, Employment Assurance Scheme (EAS), Jawahar Rozgar Yojana (JRY) and Jawahar Gram Samridhi Yojana (JGSY) funds were utilised mainly to create school buildings, health infrastructure or economic infrastructure such as roads, shops, etc. The facilities created in the villages contributed to increased economic activities. School buildings have helped in human capital formation especially for girls. Soil and moisture conservation works had an impact on the availability of work as they increased the irrigation potential and land productivity in the village. While the villagers expressed satisfaction on the construction of such works and their usefulness, it was felt that these schemes have not addressed some basic needs like availability of drinking water. Employment opportunities generated under wage employment programmes were limited, with only five to six persons in the village getting employment for around 30 days. The area development programmes, viz. the Desert Development Programme (DDP) and the Border Area Development Programme (BADP) in Pali and Jaisalmer districts have helped in meeting some of the basic needs like water. However, different works have been undertaken by different departments ignoring the advantages of complementarity of works.

Contd...

In Uttar Pradesh, a study was conducted in 20 villages in 10 districts, viz. Bareilly, Aligarh, Meerut/ Baghpat, Deoria, Jaunpur, Allahabad/Kaushambi, Fatehpur, Unnao, Hamirpur and Pithoragarh. The study revealed that during 1999-2000, some work was found to have been done in each of the villages under the employment generation programmes although the quantum varied. The most common work undertaken was earth work or *kharanja* (brick path) within the village or the construction of link roads. Panchayat buildings were constructed in some villages. Other works included installing of hand pumps, repairing of old wells for drinking water and school buildings and construction of drains. While the improvement in infrastructure enhances the development potential of the region, a very small percentage of casual labourers had benefited from the programmes. The average number of the days of employment available to the sample beneficiaries was 14.7 days only.

Source: (i) Countering Uncertainties – Strategies for Sustainable Livelihood : An Assessment of the Impact of Poverty Reduction Programmes on the Poor in Rajasthan – Institute of Development Studies, Jaipur.

(ii) Anti-Poverty Programmes in Uttar Pradesh : An Evaluation – Institute of Human Development, New Delhi.

Food for Work Programme

The Food for Work Programme was started in 2000-01 as a component of the EAS in eight notified drought-affected states of Chhattisgarh, Gujarat, Himachal Pradesh, Madhya Pradesh, Orissa, Rajasthan, Maharastra and Uttaranchal. The programme aims at augmenting food security through wage employment. Foodgrains are supplied to states free of cost. However, lifting of foodgrains for the scheme from Food Corporation of India (FCI) godowns has been slow. Against an allocation of 35.31 lakh tonnes of foodgrains, only 21.26 lakh tonnes were lifted by the target states up to January 2002. The year 2004-05 started with a much lower stock of 20 million tonnes on April 1, 2004, down from 32.8 million tonnes on April 1, 2003. Stocks, however, remained consistently higher than the buffer requirement during 2004-05 with sufficient procurement of rice and wheat and relatively lower offtake than in the previous year. On April 1, 2005, the stock at 17.40 million tonnes was above the buffer norm of 16.2 million tonnes.

Sampoorna Gramin Rozgar Yojana (SGRY)

Given the complementarity of the JGSY, EAS and Food for Work Programme, all of which aim at the creation of employment opportunities in the rural areas, they were revamped and merged under the new Sampoorna Gramin Rozgar Yojana (SGRY) from September 2001. The basic aim of the scheme continues to be generation of wage employment, creation of durable economic infrastructure in rural areas and provision of food and nutrition security to the poor. The amalgamation of the earlier schemes has led to an augmentation of resources for this programme. The works taken up under the programme are labour-intensive and the workers are paid the minimum wages notified by the states. Payment of wages is done partly in cash and partly in kind— 5 kg of foodgrains and the balance in cash. The centre and the states share the cost of the cash component of the scheme in the ratio of 75:25. An allocation of Rs. 3750 crore was made for the programme in 2001-02.

A review of various wage employment programmes during the Ninth Plan shows that there has been a considerable reduction in terms of allocation as well as in employment generation. This was largely due to changes in allocation for rural development schemes during the Plan period. The allocation by both the Centre and the states under JRY went down from Rs. 18,691 crore in the Eighth Plan to Rs. 11,688 crore in the Ninth Plan. As the EAS was launched only in 1993-94 and was intially a demand-driven scheme, it would be difficult to compare EAS allocations in the Eighth and Ninth Plan periods. However, even here it is seen that the allocations have fallen in the later half of the Ninth Plan period.

The allocation for wage employment programmes, at current prices, in the Ninth Plan was only 88 per cent of what they were in the Eighth Plan. In real terms, the allocations were much lower. A decline in allocation coupled with the increased cost of providing employment meant that as against 513 crore mandays of employment generated under JRY and EAS in the Eighth Plan, only 286 crore mandays of employment were generated under JRY/JGSY and EAS in the Ninth Plan.

The reduction in allocation for wage employment was compensated by increased allocation for some programmes and initiation of new schemes. For example, there was a substantial increase in allocation for IAY. Many other programmes taken up during the Plan period have generated employment in the rural areas. The construction of houses under IAY, programmes of rural connectivity and watershed development have fairly high employment elasticities. However, it is difficult to estimate whether these programmes were able to offset the reduction in employment generated through specific wage employment programmes.

Rural Housing

Initiated in 1985-86, the IAY is the core programme for providing free housing to BPL families in rural areas and targets SCs/STs households and freed bonded labourers. It was first merged with the JRY in 1989 and then spun off into a separate housing scheme for the rural poor in 1996. The Ninth Plan Housing Programme under IAY was framed in the light of the National Housing and Habitat Policy 1998, which set an ambitious target of providing shelter for all in the rural areas by the end of the Plan period. The allocations by the central and state governments for the programme during the Ninth Plan were substantially higher than those in the Eighth Plan. In spite of this, the housing programme under IAY has not achieved the stated objectives. As against a requirement of 109.53 lakh new and upgraded houses between 1997-98 to 2001-02, the actual construction during the period is estimated at 45 lakh houses. This, however, is a quantum jump over the Eighth Plan achievement of 26 lakh houses.

An evaluation of the IAY shows that while the programme has certainly enabled many BPL families to acquire *pucca* houses, the coverage of the beneficiaries is limited given the resource constraints. In addition, there have also been high level of leakages with a large number of non-eligible beneficiaries getting houses. The fact that houses are provided free of cost under IAY has meant that there has been virtually no progress in the other sub-schemes of IAY such as credit-cum-subsidy scheme for rural housing. This scheme, introduced in 1999-2000 to provide assistance for construction of a house to people below double the poverty line income, provides a subsidy of Rs. 10,000 and a construction loan of up to Rs. 40,000 per household. However, it failed to pick up and only 42,000 houses were constructed under the scheme between 1999 and 2001. The Samagra Awas Yojana (SAY) was taken up in 25 blocks to ensure convergence of housing, provision of safe drinking water, sanitation and common drainage facilities. The achievements under this scheme were equally unsatisfactory. A mere 30 projects have been sanctioned since the inception of the scheme and only Rs. 7.07 crore disbursed. Similarly, progress under various innovative schemes for rural housing and habitat development, which seek to encourage the use of cost-effective, environment-friendly modern designs have been equally dismal.

The Housing and Urban Development Corporation (HUDCO) has extended its activities to the rural areas, providing loans at a concessional rate of interest to economically weaker sections and low-income group households for construction of houses. HUDCO's rural housing programme was given a major boost in the Ninth Plan. The Government provided equity support for the construction of rural houses and a sum of Rs.350 crore was released to the Corporation. In the 1997-2002 period, HUDCO sanctioned 799 schemes for the construction of 50.97 lakh dwelling units at a total cost of Rs. 3991.73 crore. The regional spread of HUDCO's sanctions indicates that only Andhra Pradesh, Tamil Nadu, Karnataka, Kerala, Orissa and West Bengal took advantage of the scheme. States like Bihar, Uttar Pradesh, Madhya Pradesh, Rajasthan and Assam were not covered under the programme. One of the reasons for the lukewarm response to the scheme could be the IAY itself, which is a 100 per cent subsidy programme. Besides, HUDCO's rural housing scheme consists of a loan component and a grant component. State governments prefer the grant-based programme to the loan-based programme.

Social Security Programmes

Democratic decentralisation and centrally-supported Social Assistance Programmes were two major initiatives of the government in the 1990s. The National Social Assistance Programme (NSAP), launched in August 1995, marks a significant step towards fulfillment of the Directive Principles of State Policy. The NSAP has three components:

- National Old Age Pension Scheme (NOAPS);
- National Family Benefit Scheme (NFBS);
- National Maternity Benefit Scheme (NMBS).

The NSAP is a centrally-sponsored programme that aims at ensuring a minimum national standard of social assistance over and above the assistance that states provide from their own resources. The NOAPS provides a monthly pension of Rs. 75 to destitute BPL persons above the age of 65. The NFBS is a scheme for BPL families who are given Rs. 10,000 in the event of the death of the bread winner. The NMBS provides Rs. 500 to support nutritional intake for pregnant women. Table 6.1 provides details of expenditure and the number of beneficiaries covered under the scheme since inception.

Table: 6.1: Financial and Physical Performance under the National Social Assistance Programme

Sl.	Year	NOAPS		NFBS		NMBS	
		Expend. (Rs. crore)	No. of Beneficiaries	Expend. (Rs. crore)	No. of Beneficiaries	Expend. (Rs. crore)	No. of Beneficiaries
1.	1995-96	109.88	2,937,677	43.44	2,84,260	24.50	6,57,891
2.	1996-97	319.55	4,760,327	92.00	1,66,090	52.63	1,282,025
3.	1997-98	365.19	5,087,830	130.56	2,18,456	54.70	1,557,292
4.	1998-99	467.15	5,080,821	188.02	2,66,411	70.43	1,562,072
5.	1999-2000	456.25	5,017,542	194.98	2,15,815	73.40	1,299,719
6.	2000-01	476.66	5,148,226	200.93	2,02,999	83.90	1,456,079
7.	2001-02 (P)	362.08	5,052,568	97.96	1,04,298	Transferred to Ministry of Health and Family Welfare	

Note: (P) = Provisional.
Source: Ministry of Rural Development.

The coverage under NSAP is limited due to resource constraints. For example, against the target of 8.71 million eligible beneficiaries for old-age pension in 1999-2000, only about 5 million beneficiaries were provided assistance from central funds. Many states implement the pension scheme from their own resources. However, in the states that do not have their own scheme, a central pension of Rs. 75 per month is clearly inadequate to provide relief to old, indigent persons. A redeeming feature of the scheme, though, is that the benefits have indeed reached the poor and leakages under the scheme are low compared to many other government programmes.

In addition to NSAP, the Annapurna scheme was launched from I April 2000 to provide food security to senior citizens who were eligible for pension under NOAPS but could not receive it due to budget constraints. The scheme seeks to cover 20 per cent of persons eligible for NOAPS. These beneficiaries are given 10 kg of foodgrains per month free of cost. However, there have been major problems in the implementation of the Annapurna scheme. Haryana, Karnataka and Tamil Nadu did not agree to implement the scheme in its present form. Many other states wanted modifications before implementing it. During 2000-01, only 19,000 metric tonnes (mt) of foodgrains were lifted by ten states. As against an allocation of Rs. 99.05 crore in 2000-01, actual expenditure was only Rs. 17.44 crore. The performance in 2001-02 was equally unsatisfactory. Against a targetted coverage of 1.34 million persons, the actual coverage was only 203,000—15 per cent of the target.

Land Reforms

In an economy where over 60 per cent of the population is dependent on agriculture, the structure of land ownership is central to the well-being of the people. The government has strived to change the ownership pattern of cultivable land, but has had limited success. The abolition of intermediaries immediately after Independence, in spite of its many well-documented shortcomings and lack of implementation in certain parts of the country, was a significant achievement and covered close to 40 per cent of the cultivated area.

These achievements notwithstanding, the lack of progress in the other components of the land reforms programme, viz. implementation of land ceiling laws, security of tenure to tenants and consolidation of land holdings, remains a matter of serious concern. Agricultural workers did not benefit from the abolition of *zamindari*. The SCs/STs, who constitute the bulk of the labour force, do not have either the assets or the skills to participate in the limited but emerging employment opportunities in different sectors of the economy. The problem is further compounded by the fact that though the contribution of agriculture to GDP has nearly halved from over 50 per cent in 1951 to around 25 per cent in 2000-01, a similar transformation of employment opportunities has not taken place. The number of people dependent on agriculture and allied activities has fallen only 12 percentage points—from 71 per cent of the population in 1951 to 59 per cent in 2001.

Land reforms seem to have been relegated to the background in the 1990s. More recently, initiatives of state governments have related to liberalisation of land laws in order to promote large-scale corporate farming. This is in sharp contrast to the policy environment soon after Independence when land reforms were meant to provide ownership rights to small and marginal farmers on equity considerations. Though the pressure of population has led to sub-division and fragmentation of land holdings, thereby considerably weakening the case for further lowering of land ceilings, the need for effective implementation of the existing land ceiling laws cannot be over-emphasised. The Ninth Plan had laid strong emphasis on agrarian restructuring to make agriculture more efficient leading to increased "output and employment". However, progress on different components of the land reforms package during the Plan has been extremely limited. At the end of the Eighth Plan, 74.9 lakh acres was declared as ceiling surplus and 52.13 lakh acres was distributed among 5.5 million beneficiaries. By the end of the Ninth Plan, the position was virtually the same. There has been no progress in the detection of concealed land and its distribution to the landless rural poor.

The case of tenancy reforms is equally unsatisfactory. Tenancy laws in the states follow different patterns, as land is a state subject. Several states, including Uttar Pradesh, Bihar and Orissa have either banned tenancy completely or have imposed such restrictive conditions that land leases are virtually impossible. Studies by the Lal Bahadur Shastri National Academy of Administration indicate that this has only resulted in concealed tenancy. It is estimated that over 34 per cent of land is operated under concealed tenancy in Bihar. The ban on tenancy, which was meant to protect tenants, has only ended up hurting the economic interests of the tenants as they are not even recognised as tenants. As a result, they are denied the benefits of laws that provide security of tenure and regulate rent.

The progress on the consolidation of land holdings has also been slow. Consolidation has to be a continuing process, but most states have stopped consolidation proceedings. As on 31 March, 2002, consolidation of holdings has taken place only in an area of 66.10 million hectares against a total cultivable area of 142 million hectares.

Alienation of tribals from their land is a major issue in tribal areas. States have passed legislation to restore alienated land to the tribal landholders. The progress in this regard, however, has been limited. The restoration proceedings have been challenged in courts, thwarting the restoration of land to tribals. During the Ninth Plan period, 1.63 lakh cases were decided by the courts in favour of the tribals and 1,75,286 hectares (ha) were restored as a result of the governmental action. However, as on 31 March 2002, 57,521 cases were still pending in courts with 58,260 ha being under dispute in these cases.

A land record management system is a pre-condition for an effective land reform programme. In 1987-88, a centrally-sponsored scheme for Strengthening of Revenue Administration and Updating of Land Records (SRA & ULR) was introduced in Orissa and Bihar. The scheme was extended to other states in 1989-90. Survey and re-settlement operations, pre-service and in-service training to revenue and settlement staff, facilities for modernisation of survey and settlement operations and strengthening of revenue machinery at the village level are funded under the scheme. During the Eighth Plan, Rs. 8.23 crore was released to the states under the scheme, while Rs. 92.60 crore was allocated during the Ninth Plan under the Programme of

SRA & ULR against which Rs. 85.74 crore was released to States/Union Territories.

In addition to SRA & ULR, a centrally-sponsored scheme of Computerisation of Land Records (CLR) provides assistance to states for modernisation of record keeping operations. Activities funded under the programme include the screening and digitalisation of existing cadastral maps, computer processing of agricultural land holdings records for the purpose of consolidation of holdings and preparation of consolidated revenue settlement and installation of computer networks at the headquarters of States/Union Territories for revenue administration. During the Eighth Plan period, Rs. 9.42 crore was released to the state governments for covering 238 districts. In the Ninth Plan, 333 more districts were brought under the scheme, thus taking the total districts covered under CLR to 571 districts. A total of 2705 talukas/tehsils/ blocks were taken up for computerisation. Against a total allocation of Rs. 178 crore, a sum of Rs. 167.52 crore was released. The resources provided under SRA & ULR and CLR programmes meet a small part of the total resources required for the modernisation of revenue administration. The states have to undertake modernisation of the land records management system on a much larger scale.

Strategy for the Tenth Plan

The Approach Paper to the Tenth Plan set a target for reduction of poverty and creation of high quality gainful employment during the Plan period. With the GDP growth rate of 8 per cent for the period 2002-07, it aimed at reduction of incidence of poverty by 5 percentage points by 2007. Compared to 1999-2000, poverty is expected to decline by 15 percentage points by 2011-12. Effective implementation of anti-poverty programmes would be central to achieving the planned reductions in poverty. The challenge before the State is to provide employment opportunities which provide enhanced incomes. This becomes more important in view of the fact that substantial additions to labour force are expected to take place during the next five years. Enlargement of self and wage-employment programmes and their effective delivery becomes imperative in such a scenario.

Self Employment Programmes

The coverage of beneficiaries in the Ninth Plan was considerably lower than the coverage under SGSY. The formation of self-help groups by itself contributes to the empowerment and economic well-being of the poor by improving their collective bargaining position. The group formation also emphasises social capital and enables the poor to interact with other social groups from a position of strength. Group formation would continue to be the focus under the SGSY. The self-help groups move through various stages: social mobilisation and formation of groups (initial phase); savings and internal lending among the members of the group on their own, augmented by revolving fund grants from the government and linkages with banks and other credit agencies (second phase); obtaining micro-finance (third phase) and setting up of micro-enterprises (fourth phase). This is a long process and groups require time to mature as cohesive units.

Savings by members and internal lending help the group members to improve their economic position. A strong group acts as collateral for banks to provide micro-finance to these groups. They get access to credit for a variety of consumption needs, seasonal activities and for undertaking petty production and trading activities. Setting up of a micro-enterprise could be the objective of every group. However, only those groups which possess special skills, technical know-how, establish marketing linkages and have access to the essential infrastructure needed for success of that particular activity can reach the stage of micro-enterprise. The IRDP's approach of fixing targets and time frames was given up under the SGSY in the Ninth Plan itself. This approach continued in the Tenth Plan too.

The SGSY programme is intended to provide benefits to SCs and STs, disabled and women-headed households which form the bulk of the rural poor. However, these sections would be excluded from the ambit of the programme if they are not listed in the below poverty line (BPL) census conducted at the beginning of every Five-Year Plan for inclusion of beneficiaries under different government programmes. Greater attention would, therefore, be given to identification of BPL families by clearly specifying exclusion and inclusion criteria. These would be published and subjected to periodic social audit in a transparent manner by the gram sabhas.

Self-help groups become cohesive in the long run only if they are homogenous. Social mobilisation is an important step in the formation of self-help groups. It requires a high degree of motivation, morale, expertise, management skills, time and pro-poor orientation on the part of the person who acts as a catalyst for group formation. SGSY is implemented through the DRDAs. These organisations would have to be supported by NGOs, PRIs and other community-based organisations in the formation of the self-help groups. The Small Industries Development Bank of India (SIDBI), National Bank of Agriculture and Rural Development (NABARD), Rashtriya Mahila Kosh (RMK) and many zila parishads have emerged as important players in the promotion of self-help groups. Strong networks and linkages would be established with such institutions under SGSY. These organisations would act as self-help promotion institutions and would ensure a continuing relationship with self-help groups.

Successful experiments in the promotion of micro-finance and micro-enterprise have revealed a strong partnership between NGOs and financial institutions. NGOs have an inherent advantage in reaching the poor due to their proximity, the trust they generate by working in the area, their commitment, flexibility in approach, responsiveness and cost-effectiveness. They have played a dynamic role as social animators and organisers in rural areas. Many NGOs have not only been instrumental in the formation of self-help groups but have also nurtured them over the years. Such NGOs have a strong presence in many states. However, voluntary and non-governmental action is weak in some of the poorer states. These are also the states where the spirit of cooperation and collaboration may be lacking because of poverty itself. Training of social animators would have to be promoted in such states. Departments of social sciences, social work, agriculture and rural development in universities and colleges could be engaged as facilitators in the process of group formation so that every rural habitation has at least one self-help group by the end of 2004. The institutions which promote self-help groups could be provided remuneration at different stages of the evolution of the groups so that they have an incentive in the formation of cohesive groups and in ensuring their success.

Micro-enterprises succeed only if they cater to the specific needs of an area. The identification of key activities and planning of activity clusters is an important component of SGSY though it has been a weak link so far. It is necessary to identify livelihood opportunities, the constraints in the realisation of these opportunities and the investments that would have to be made to remove these constraints. The micro-level planning process would have to be strengthened in the districts for the programme to succeed. In this endeavour, the involvement of PRIs, banks, micro-finance institutions, NGOs and district-level officers of different departments would have to be ensured. They would have to work in close coordination in the preparation of a District Plan for activities under SGSY.

Economic activities require high degree of skills. After the identification of key activities, it would be necessary to organise training programmes for upgrading skills of beneficiaries selected under the programme. Skill acquisition is a long-drawn process; this requires not only short-term training in campus-based programmes, but also on-the-job training in existing enterprises. Campus-based training programmes under SGSY would only be a beginning of the process. The design of the curricula and method of training would have to correspond to the activities chosen. A basic foundation course to expose trainees to accounting procedures, management techniques, banking and marketing would be a part of the training programme. The training institutions would be expected to arrange for practical on-the-job training programmes and upgrade their syllabi in tune with changing market conditions. They would be continuously appraised to ensure that their faculty is well qualified and imparts training which is relevant and of high quality. They would also be expected to monitor the progress of their trainees in the trades that they pursue.

It would be necessary for training institutions to forge partnerships with technical and management institutes to facilitate greater interaction and learning. In the coming years, the corporate sector is expected to play a larger role in the rural areas. Industry associations have indicated their willingness to adopt villages and regions. The corporate sector could associate itself with training institutes, enabling the latter to keep abreast of the market requirements and revise their curricula. The trainees could also set up ancillary units to supply components to industry.

The SGSY programme would be credit driven. The outreach of the credit delivery system in the country continues to be limited, despite several measures to streamline it. The legitimate demands for credit remain unfulfilled as a vast majority of the poor remain outside the purview of the formal credit system. The mismatch between demand and supply of credit arises out of an inadequate and inefficient delivery system. The policies of direct lending, administered pricing of credit and lack of freedom in the selection of borrowers have resulted in the high cost of credit delivery for the formal credit institutions and, consequently, to the borrowers. A system would have to be put in place which is flexible and responsive to the financial needs of the poor and is capable of supplying timely and adequate credit.

The inadequacies of formal credit institutions could be overcome by combining the strength of commercial banks with the intermediation capabilities of NGOs to effectively link the poor with the commercial banking channels. This would be a cost-effective alternative for providing credit to the poor as banks would be able to reach a larger number of small borrowers with lower transaction costs. The risk of default on loans would be lower due to group pressure and the groups would also monitor the end use of credit. Access to banks through self-help groups would reduce the transaction cost of the borrowers. In the credit delivery system under SGSY, financial intermediation by NGOs would be encouraged. The experience of Self Employed Women's Association (SEWA) and other organisations would be replicated on a larger scale.

Since the commercial banking network has its limitations in reaching the rural poor in every part of the country, other formal institutions that cater to the specific credit needs of the rural population could be integrated into the credit delivery structure for self-employment programmes. Primary Agriculture Credit Cooperative Societies (PACS) have an extensive network in the country and possess detailed knowledge of the borrowers. Regional Rural Banks (RRBs) and other credit organisations, presently outside the purview of micro-finance activities, could be associated with self-employment programmes.

It would be the Government's endeavour to leverage funds under different self-employment programmes to enable the rural poor to diversify into non-agricultural activities. Different government agencies have, in the past, attempted to promote rural non-farm employment. Khadi and Village Industries Commission (KVIC) and District Industries Centres (DICs) were set up to promote non-farm activities. In spite of this, the rural non-farm sector continues to lag behind. Only 16 per cent of the rural population is engaged in non-farm activities and that too largely in village or cottage enterprises. Economic census data shows that 77 per cent of rural enterprises are own account enterprises that do not engage hired labour. These enterprises are unable to attract capital and technology since they are small, family-based enterprises. Many of these enterprises use obsolete technology and are highly vulnerable to market fluctuations and competition from the organised sector.

The inadequate availability of micro-infrastructure relevant to the service or trade has been a major constraint in the rapid development of the rural non-farm sector. For example, dairy activity was one of the main activities financed under IRDP. Often the beneficiaries were constrained by the absence of small equipment like milk cans and fat testing machines. Provision of milk collection vans, bulk coolers, chilling plants and pasteurisation facilities were also not a part of the programme. There is, therefore, a need to identify the type of infrastructure required for a particular activity while planning an activity cluster. Provision would have to be made for the creation of infrastructure either under SGSY or by convergence with the other sectoral programmes and to ensure that the missing infrastructure is provided at the planning stage itself.

Marketing strategy is an integral part of every self-employment venture. Market intelligence has to be developed. Survey of local and urban markets to understand product demand is necessary. Rural *haats* or village markets have to be set up to position the products of self-help groups. Such *haats* would also be promoted at the taluka level, district centres and other larger towns. The construction of permanent spaces and *pucca* sheds along with the provision of storage facilities/ godowns would be taken up under SGSY and transport links provided to such centres. Metropolitan cities and export markets are important from the point of view of higher value realisation. Linkages to these would have to be developed largely through private channels, industrial enterprises and export houses. This model was successfully demonstrated in Andhra Pradesh where Phillips India and Hindustan Lever had forged links with DWCRA groups for marketing their products. Intermediate aggregate mechanisms like producer cooperatives and marketing agencies could facilitate the transaction between dispersed producers and industrial enterprises/export houses.

Products would be positioned through KVIC outlets, State Emporia and Handlooms and Handicrafts Trade Fairs. SGSY groups from a cluster of villages could also form a federation. Such federations, producing a single product, can take advantage of the economies of scale, undertaking collective purchase of raw materials to reduce the cost of production. They could ensure better marketing, quality control and promote their brand name through aggressive advertisement campaigns. Greater attention to quality control, standardisation and packaging would be required for products of rural areas to find a market in the urban centres. Efforts would be made to create a market niche for rural products that require specialised skills.

Rural enterprises need technology support for product development, quality improvement and standardisation. India has large research and development facilities in national laboratories, universities and other specialised institutions. Suitable linkages between the rural enterprises and these institutions would be developed so that technological assistance can be extended to the self-help groups. Advances in information technology and communication would be harnessed to benefit the self-help groups.

Self-employment programmes are likely to have an uneven regional spread, succeeding in areas that have a tradition of artisanship, developed road and rail infrastructure, banking facilities and a skilled human resource base. The negative relationship between the incidence of rural poverty and land access is well-established. The landless face the greatest risk of poverty. Access to even small pieces of land which may not be sufficient for providing income to a family for subsistence can significantly reduce poverty and food insecurity by providing an essential component in a diversified livelihood system. Their impact may be less visible in underdeveloped, backward and tribal regions. The SGSY programme would continue to promote land-based activities for individual and group beneficiaries in the backward regions. Diversification into other land-based activities such as sericulture, aquaculture, horticulture and floriculture would be encouraged. The programme would, therefore, support the purchase of land and its distribution to the landless rural poor. Women *swarozgaris* would be sole owners or joint owners of redistributed land. The *swarozgaris* provided land would be organised to access inputs and credit facilities that enhance productivity of land. In addition to the provision for purchase and redistribution of land, self-help groups will be encouraged to explore prospects of leasing or purchasing land in joint ownership. Schemes that give subsidised credit for land purchase and leasing would be converged with the SGSY programme in these areas. Convergence would also be attempted with schemes that provide subsidised credit for farm equipment such as tractors, tube-wells, fertilisers, seeds and other inputs. The Government would make special efforts to provide information and give financial and infrastructural support to SGSY groups engaged in land-based activities in such areas.

In the Ninth Plan, both IRDP and SGSY were subsidy-driven programmes. This subsidy itself has become a major obstacle in the promotion of self-employment ventures. The experience of institutions providing micro-finance shows that the poor are capable and also willing to pay for the credit and other financial services rendered by NGOs and financial institutions without depending on the government for subsidy. Financial resources in the Tenth Plan, therefore, would be directed towards providing infrastructure and other support facilities which increase the returns to households and reduce their risks. It would be used in innovative ways to lower the transaction cost for both the *swarozgaris* and the lenders and to create a strong and viable partnership with NGOs and other organisations working for the economic well-being of the rural poor.

Wage Employment Programme

The SGRY would be the single wage employment programme. Allocations to the programme would be stepped up. The programme would seek to provide productive employment opportunities in employment-intensive sectors. The Government would endeavour to generate a shelf of projects for execution under SGRY that fits into the overall development plan of an area.

The SGRY would have three streams. One to address the need for rural infrastructure in all states; the other to provide focused attention to areas facing endemic poverty while the third would respond to natural calamities. The general stream universalised across states would be for the creation of local infrastructure. Water tanks, *anganwadis*, primary school buildings, sanitation facilities, primary health centres, multi-purpose community halls and other projects that are required in the village would be taken up under the universal stream. In agriculturally developed areas, it may be necessary to allow upward adjustments in wages to attract unskilled labour. Village communities could augment the resources under the universal stream by mobilising contributions from within the community.

The second stream would seek to provide an employment guarantee of at least 100 days for areas facing chronic unemployment and poverty. The districts and blocks would be selected on the basis of an objective criterion and efforts would be made to create at least minimum infrastructure in these areas by ensuring convergence of other government programmes. Thus, the second stream would, in essence, correspond to the EAS, which was started with the objective of providing employment for 100 days in drought-prone, desert-prone, hilly and flood-prone blocks of the country. Such an assurance would ensure a minimum level of employment and stability to the incomes of the poor and give them an opportunity to develop their collective strength. It would improve their economic position, reduce vulnerability and discourage migration to facilitate their continued access to health, education and welfare facilities available in the village. The allocation under this second stream would be enhanced to meet the target of 100 days of employment for every able-bodied person willing and seeking work.

The third stream would be an enabling mechanism for the Government to respond to natural calamities such as floods, droughts, earthquakes and other contingencies that require quick response to mitigate the hardships faced by people.

The wage employment programmes provide only short-term relief to the poor. Long-term sustainable poverty reduction in the underdeveloped regions can come about only if other sectors of the economy grow rapidly. It is imperative, therefore, to ensure that the growth process is inclusive and pro-poor. Agricultural growth still holds the key to poverty alleviation in the Indian context. There is considerable scope for increasing agricultural productivity through expansion of irrigation, better land and water management practices and infrastructure support. The planning of works under the SGRY would be undertaken keeping this in mind.

A large number of rural facilities have been built under various programmes over successive Plan periods. However, they have degenerated either due to their initial faulty design and construction, or lack of maintenance. Therefore, a specific proportion of allocations under SGRY would be used for the maintenance of assets.

PRIs would play a major role in the planning, implementation and monitoring of wage employment programmes and allocations under the SGRY would be routed through them. A rational criterion would have to be evolved for distribution of funds between the three tiers of the PRIs to ensure balanced development of villages, blocks and districts.

Rural Housing

As noted earlier, though the IAY is one of the successful programmes being implemented by the Ministry of Rural Development, it has certain weaknesses. The provision of free houses has meant that other loan-based schemes have not been able to take off. The scheme has also been open to misuse. Public funds have to be utilised for the promotion of economic activity and growth. The creation of employment opportunities, both self-employment and wage-employment, has to receive a higher priority than provision of free houses. During the Tenth Plan period, free houses under IAY would be provided largely to SC/ST BPL families. For other BPL families, there would be a gradual shift to a credit-linked housing programme.

There is a need to create institutional capability in the rural housing sector with reference to designing of houses, supply of raw materials and construction. The rural communities have to be involved in the layout and design of the houses. The houses should have provisions for rain water harvesting, water supply and sanitation.

Social Security Schemes

While the NSAP and state-level welfare schemes have provided some succour to the poor in the form of assistance to the old and the bereaved, a large section of people have not been covered under the schemes because of limited resources. The NSAP needs to be enlarged in scope to cover all eligible beneficiaries. The content and coverage of the social welfare scheme would have to be strengthened during the Plan period to provide meaningful protection to the poor. There are a plethora of welfare schemes in both the central and state sectors. They lead to avoidable overlap and confusion and need to rationalised. Since welfare is basically a state subject, these schemes are best administered by state governments. The NSAP has been transferred to states with earmarked funds in the Tenth Plan.

Land Reforms

Successive Five-Year Plans have addressed the issue of secure rights in land for increased agricultural productivity under the land reforms programme. Land reform legislations, besides abolishing intermediaries and providing ownership rights to farmers, also provided for security of tenure to tenants and regulation of rent. Actual cultivators were brought into a direct relationship with the state. The abolition of intermediaries succeeded in providing ownership rights to a large number of tenants. The advent of the green revolution technology coupled with schemes of asset transfer under IRDP have contributed significantly to the increased incomes not only from agricultural operations but also on account of diversification into animal husbandry.

Agricultural workers, however, did not gain from *zamindari* abolition. Scheduled Castes and Scheduled Tribes constitute bulk of the agricultural labour force. These people have neither assets nor skills to participate in the limited but emerging employment opportunities in different sectors of the economy. The problem is further compounded by the fact that employment opportunities in non-farm sector have not increased over time to absorb the rural labour force.

Ownership of even a small plot of land enables a family to raise its income, improve its nutritional status, have access to credit facilities and lead a more dignified life. Studies of economies of scale in farm operations show that modern agricultural technology is scale neutral in the case of a majority of food and cereal crops which the poor tend to grow. Horticulture, floriculture and vegetable cultivation on small plots of land, including homestead lands, have proved beneficial for the poor. Agricultural labourers, therefore, need to be provided access to land to improve their economic and social well-being.

The scope for lowering land ceilings, which were fixed in 1972, and redistribution of surplus land is limited. The total area declared ceiling surplus after 1972 was less than 2 per cent of the net sown area. National Sample Survey Organisation (NSSO) data for 1992 shows that 72 per cent of rural households had less than one hectare of land. Therefore, further reduction in land ceilings and acquisition of land for distribution to the poor is not a credible policy option any more. However, this is not to underplay the need to acquire the land declared ceiling surplus. The record of most states in implementing the existing laws is dismal. Concealment of land is widespread. Land acquisitions have been disputed, with cases piled up in courts for years without resolution. During the Tenth Plan period, states have to concentrate on the detection of concealed land and strive for the speedy disposal of cases so that the land acquired under ceiling laws becomes available for distribution to the poor.

The reform of tenancy in the post-Independence period was taken up as a part of the land reforms agenda. Its basic thrust was to stop eviction of tenants and fixation of rent. Conferment of ownership rights to the tenants was the ultimate goal of tenancy laws. The policy attempted to reconcile twin objectives of protection to existing tenants and resumption of land for personal cultivation by the medium, small and marginal farmers. However, the prohibition of tenancy has not really ended the practice. On the other hand, it has resulted in agricultural practices that are not conducive to increased production. This, in turn, also depresses employment opportunities for the landless agricultural labourers. Mechanisation of agriculture has enabled families to keep land under personal cultivation even in the absence of able-bodied persons to take care of agricultural operations. The fear of tenant eventually taking possession of the land in these areas has resulted in agricultural practices which are not conducive to increased agricultural production. This, in turn depresses employment opportunities for the landless agricultural labourers.

The changes in the agrarian economy over the past three decades warrant a fresh look at tenancy laws. States are at different stages of agricultural transformation. Patterns of semi-feudal agriculture in some states co-exist with corporate and commercial farming practices in others. Where agriculture has reached the commercial farming stage, middle and large farmers lease land from small and marginal farmers. NSSO surveys show that area owned by the marginal and small farmers is greater than the area they cultivate. These developments indicate the need to revisit the tenancy laws.

One option could be to completely free tenancy laws of all restrictive conditions. Farmers owning land below the ceiling limit may be provided a guarantee that their land would not be taken away. The fixation of rent could be left to the market forces. Given the extent of concealed tenancy in states that have banned tenancy, it is not likely to increase area under tenancy dramatically in the short run. However, in the medium to long run, more land would be expected to come on the land lease market which can be accessed by the rural poor.

Civil society organisations have attempted innovative experiments to rectify inequities of land ownership in the rural areas. Access to land for the landless has been built into their programmes. The Pani Panchayat in Ralegaon Siddhi in Maharashtra is a case in point. Every member of the village has a proprietary right over the harvested water. Every member, irrespective of the size of his land holding, has a share in the harvested water for irrigation. As the water available to each member is limited, members with large land holdings have been persuaded to lease their land to small and marginal farmers and agricultural labourers who have water rights but no land. The arrangement has allowed landless access to land. The large land holders have also benefited as they receive rent for land which would otherwise have remained fallow for lack of irrigation.

Another variant of this approach has been adopted in a few watersheds. While the land holders get water for irrigation, the non-land owning families get a larger share of output from the Common Property Resources (CPRs) which get rejuvenated after the successful completion of the project. This has enabled many families to take up animal husbandry as an occupation and meet their fodder and fuel requirements from the CPRs. Fishing rights on ponds constructed as part of the watershed project are only given to self-help groups of the landless. These arrangements effectively increase the access of the poor to the land and other sources of livelihood and improve their standard of living.

Successful projects change the nature of agricultural land from unirrigated to irrigated. In such cases, the ceiling laws of the state could come into force and the ceiling surplus land could be distributed to the landless poor. Alternatively, the guidelines for watershed development projects could be modified to give priority to those watershed projects where the village community, through a resolution, agrees to provide land access to the landless labourers on a continuing basis.

In addition, outright purchase of land from farmers willing to sell their holdings also needs to be explored. In many parts of the country, families have migrated to urban areas but continue to hold on to their land holdings in the absence of an efficient land market due to restrictions on the lease, sale and mortgage of agricultural land. The Government could create an enabling environment for the emergence of land markets or itself enter the land market as a major player. The National Scheduled Castes and Scheduled Tribes Finance and Development Corporation (NSFDC) has a scheme for providing assistance to SC/ST families to purchase land. The scheme received an enthusiastic response in Tamil Nadu, Andhra Pradesh and Karnataka (Box 6.3).

Box 6.3
Land Purchase Scheme

The NSFDC, set up in 1989, has emerged as a major promoter of economic activities for SC/ST families living below double the poverty line limits. The Corporation finances state agencies working for the development of the SCs/STs. It also finances individuals for setting up enterprises. The Corporation financed the Land Purchase Scheme for the first time in Tamil Nadu in 1991. The driving force behind the scheme were two NGOs – Land For Tillers Freedom (LAFTI) and Dr. Ambedkar Peoples' Society (DAPSY) – which organised people in the Thanjavur district to secure land to the tillers through democratic means.

The two organisations identified land owners willing to sell land as well as SC/ST families who were to be provided land after acquisition. The project was appraised and sanctioned by the NSFDC which released money through the Tamil Nadu Adi Dravidar Housing and Development Corporation (TADHCO). Part of the project cost was funded by the IRDP subsidy.

LAFTI purchased 951.33 acres of land and distributed it to 1,018 landless SC/ST families at a total cost of Rs. 71.29 lakh. DAPSY purchased 556.64 acres of land and distributed it to 550 families. A subsidy of Rs. 28.03 lakh was provided under IRDP for LAFTI beneficiaries. Subsidy was made available to DAPSY beneficiaries also. The land rights were given either solely to women or jointly with their husbands. The land was mortgaged to TADHCO for an initial period of 10 years and TADHCO charged 6 per cent interest for the loan provided to the beneficiaries. Ownership rights were to be restored after the loan was repaid.

The scheme was later appraised by the Agricultural Finance Corporation Ltd (AFCL). It concluded that the status of the beneficiaries had improved after they acquired land. The project had a far-reaching social impact. The average income of the beneficiaries increased considerably, with family incomes almost doubling. As a result, 45 per cent of the beneficiary families had crossed the poverty line. The asset retention was close to 98 per cent. The families were able to take up dairy activity as a result of their access to land. There were, however, some problems in the repayment of loans, especially in the case of DAPSY beneficiaries since their loan amount was higher than that of LAFTI beneficiaries.

The NSFDC has sanctioned similar projects in Andhra Pradesh and Karnataka. Though it has sanctioned schemes in other states, the coverage of beneficiaries is extremely limited. Given the changes that are taking place in the agrarian sector and the migration of people to urban centres in search of better opportunities, land purchase could emerge as an attractive proposition for providing land to the landless.

Source: National Scheduled Caste Finance and Development Corporation.

While the provision for purchase of land in the erstwhile IRDP continues in the revamped SGSY, the main focus of the scheme is on the creation of self-help groups and setting up of micro-enterprises. Land could be purchased and distributed to landless under SGSY and they could be organised under a cooperative society to provide other support services for agricultural operations.

There has been an increasing feminisation of the agricultural labour force in the country. NSSO (50th round) estimates for 1993-94 show that 75.3 per cent of women workers were engaged in agriculture compared to only 58 per cent of male workers. In the rural labour force, 84.7 per cent of women were engaged in agriculture as compared to 73.8 per cent male workers. Data on incremental additions to the rural labour force show that the rural male worker has a greater chance of getting absorbed into non-agriculture pursuits than the rural female worker. Besides, migration of able-bodied men to urban areas in search of employment, break-up of the joint family system and other social factors such as death of husbands and desertion by husbands have resulted in an increase in the number of female-headed households. However, in the case of land holding families headed by women, if male descendants are present, the ownership right does not devolve on the women. Protecting social cohesion and prevention of fragmentation of land holdings are some of the major arguments advanced against allowing women to inherit land. These gender-biased land laws put women-headed households at a disadvantage. Without proper title to land, they are denied access to credit and other facilities available to farming communities. This not only affects the income generating capacity of the households but also impacts adversely on agricultural production. Therefore, both on grounds of equity and efficiency, land inheritance laws need to be gender neutral.

Alienation of Tribal Lands

The influx of non-tribals into tribal areas as a result of various developmental projects, exploitation of natural resources and industrial activities has led to the alienation of tribal land. It is extremely paradoxical that while outsiders/non-tribals have come into the Scheduled Areas in the name of development, the local tribal population gets displaced and migrate to urban areas in search of employment. This has given rise to severe discontent in the tribal areas.

The process of alienation has taken place because of lack of legal awareness about land rights among both tribals and government officials and ineffective administrative structures. Inherent deficiencies in legal provisions such as the absence of any machinery to initiate *suo motu* action, general period of limitation for adverse possession, lack of provision against trespass and against fraudulent and collusive transfer of land to non-tribals continue to exist. Alienation has also been facilitated by improper land records. An in-depth scrutiny of the methods for preparation of land records, and the maintenance and updating of such records must, therefore, be carried out at the earliest. Computerisation of land records in tribal areas should also be accorded the highest priority.

The Panchayats (Extension of Scheduled Areas) Act (PESA), 1996 extended the provisions of 73rd Constitutional Amendment Act, 1992, to the Scheduled Areas in the states of Andhra Pradesh, Chhattisgarh, Gujarat, Himachal Pradesh, Jharkhand, Madhya Pradesh, Maharashtra, Orissa and Rajasthan. The PESA enables tribals to assume control over their own destiny and to preserve and conserve their traditional rights over natural resources, including land. However, the stringent provisions of this law have remained only on paper and have not been operationalised by state governments. PESA was proposed to be effectively implemented during the Tenth Plan period to resolve the issues of tribal exploitation and alienation.

One of the main reasons for the concealment of land, which has hampered the land reforms programme, has been the lack of a comprehensive land rights database. The CLR and SRA&ULR schemes have placed emphasis on modernisation of cadastral survey procedures and strengthening of training facilities for revenue, survey and settlement staff. Provision of computers and other infrastructure has been made under these schemes. This process will be carried forward more vigorously in the Tenth Plan not only to detect concealment of land but also to reduce scope for litigation in rural areas.

Delivery Mechanism

Poverty alleviation programmes have been designed to address different facets of rural poverty. Micro credit-linked programmes provide a package of services including credit and subsidy to set up micro-enterprises. Wage employment programmes address the issue of transient poverty. Besides, schemes for infrastructure development and provision of basic services contribute to the well-being of the rural people. Successful implementation of these programmes requires an appropriate policy framework, adequate funds, and an effective delivery mechanism. Past experience shows that the mere availability of funds is not likely to eradicate rural poverty. Nor is the design of the rural development programmes, no matter how refined, a sufficient condition. The success of these programmes ultimately depends on the capability of the delivery system to absorb and utilise the funds in a cost-effective manner. An effective and responsive district-level field machinery with a high degree of commitment, motivation, professional competence and, above all, integrity has been recognised as one of the prerequisites for successful implementation of anti-poverty programmes.

An effective delivery system has to ensure people's participation at various stages of the formulation and implementation of the programmes, transparency in the operation of the schemes and adequate monitoring. International experience shows that greater functional and financial devolution to local governments results in higher allocation of resources for social sectors and more efficient use of resources. Such trends in social spending have been witnessed in many Indian states as well.

The increasing integration of India in the global economy, the budget constraints faced by both central and state governments and inefficiencies in the administrative structure led to the development of a consensus to devolve powers to local institutions to enable people's participation in administration. The 73rd and 74th Constitutional Amendments that conferred statutory status on PRIs and urban local bodies did not have only democratic decentralisation as their objective. These institutions were also seen as a process for harnessing and channelising the people's innate abilities to bring about rural transformation in a way that every individual acquired his/her rightful place in the social, economic and political arena.

The Ninth Plan had called for the devolution of functional responsibilities, administrative control on government functionaries dealing with subjects listed in the Eleventh Schedule of the Constitution and financial resources for taking up developmental programmes to the PRIs. There has been mixed progress on this front. Political devolution has taken place. Elections have been held and women, SCs/STs and other marginalised groups have got political representation in the rural areas. Problems encountered in the process of evolution of panchayats have been taken care of with the intervention of courts, civil society organisations and increased public awareness. The strengthening of forces that facilitate political empowerment of rural communities was proposed be an important area of action in the Tenth Plan period. Issues of transparency, accountability and development would require greater attention. States which have lagged behind in devolving functions and finances to panchayats were proposed to be encouraged to empower the panchayats.

The gram sabhas in most states have been entrusted with only ceremonial functions. The power and functions of gram sabhas need to be enlarged by giving them effective powers of implementation and monitoring of developmental plans. Social audit of all development programmes by the gram sabha would be made mandatory. The committee system adopted in many states to facilitate a more participative decision-making process in the panchayats should be incorporated in the State Panchayat Acts. The powers entrusted to a gram sabha in a Scheduled V area could be extended to gram sabhas in non-scheduled areas as well.

Administrative and financial devolution by the states to the PRIs remains an area of major concern. The Constitution has placed onerous responsibilities on PRIs. They require financial resources to discharge the tasks assigned to them and emerge as viable institutions of self-government. Financial devolution is also desirable as the control of investment decisions by local communities leads to better utilisation of scarce resources. Panchayats would need greater powers of taxation and avenues for non-tax revenue. States could provide matching grants to panchayats to take up specific projects. Apart from the funds that flow to panchayats for centrally sponsored and state sector schemes, untied grants could also be provided to the PRIs. The PRIs need to raise resources from the local community and end their dependence on government funds. The functional domain of the PRIs can be enlarged only if they pay adequate attention to their resource base.

The onus for devolving functions, functionaries and financial resources to the PRIs rests with the state governments. Though the states have, slowly, transferred functions and finances to the PRIs, these institutions are hampered by lack of administrative support. PRIs have to be adequately staffed and the functionaries must be trained in planning, budgeting and accounting tasks. An elaborate system for auditing of panchayat finances has to be put in place. At present, adequate safeguards against the misuse of resources by elected functionaries do not exist in many states. These issues need to be tackled on a priority basis.

The 74th Constitutional Amendment Act provided for the constitution of District Planning Committees (DPCs). However, the Constitutional provision on DPCs is rather weak as it provides for the preparation of only draft Plans by the DPCs. State governments have not given adequate attention to the DPCs and the Government of India's guidelines on district planning have not been fully operationalised. DPCs should be set up and its functionaries must be trained in the basics of planning. The gram sabha/panchayat should be associated with the preparation of village development Plans based on the felt needs of the people. These Plans should be integrated with the panchayat samiti and district-level plans to make the grassroot planning process a reality in the Tenth Plan period.

The voluntary sector has witnessed a phenomenal growth in the country in the last 20 years. These institutions have played an important role in community mobilisation, providing technical support to the community for developmental projects, especially in the areas of health and education. It has been clearly established that where panchayats, community organisations and user groups have worked in close cooperation, people have benefited immensely from developmental projects initiated either by the government or the communities themselves. People's organisations, whether in the form of an NGO or a group of experts, provide expertise and competence to the panchayats that they otherwise may not possess. However, in many places, the emergence of constitutionally-mandated PRIs has led to a conflict of interest as both voluntary organisations and these institutions occupy the same space. The voluntary agencies have to recognise that PRIs are institutions of governance and must work in close cooperation with them. The PRIs, for their part, have to recognise the critical role that voluntary organisations can play in enhancing their capabilities.

The delivery of programmes would improve only if the PRIs emerge as strong players in the social and economic life of the country. NGOs and other civil society organisations can facilitate the evolution of PRIs as institutions geared to promote the well-being of the rural poor.

The preceding paragraphs have described the content and direction of anti-poverty programmes in the Tenth Plan period. The financial allocations for the Tenth Plan period for these programmes have been stepped up considerably. As against a total expenditure of Rs. 35,866 crore in the Ninth Plan, the allocation for the Tenth Plan period was increased to Rs. 56,748 crore. Resources for the SGRY and for rural connectivity under Pradhan Mantri Gram Sadak Yojana (PMGSY) have been substantially enhanced. These are expected to provide assured wage-employment, enhance incomes and ensure nutritional security. The allocations for direct anti-poverty alleviation programmes would be complemented by investments in other sectors which have a strong bearing on the incidence of poverty.

The Path Ahead

Rural poverty alleviation programmes were revamped and re-focused during the Ninth Plan to increase their effectiveness. Programmes that provide self-employment and wage employment to the poor were emphasised greatly in the Tenth Plan.

- SGSY would provide opportunities for self-employment to the rural poor. The programme would shift to a process-oriented approach in four stages.
    - Social mobilisation for formation of self help groups;
    - Savings among the group and internal lending among its members and provision of a revolving fund;

  - Micro-finance; and
  - Micro-enterprise development.
- Network of institutions that promote the self-help movement was proposed to be created during the Plan period. Partnership was envisaged to be forged between NGOs and other community-based organisations, government agencies and other financial institutions. There would be a system of identifying and training local facilitators.
- Key activities were to be planned to respond to the needs of the area. Training programmes for beneficial linkages with training institutions were to be forged.
- Greater attention was to be paid to marketing. Rural *haats*/markets at the taluka/district level were to be set up for display of products. Linkages were to be developed with private channels, industrial enterprises and export houses for higher value realisation for SGSY groups.
- Special attention was to be paid to provide technical support for upgrading technology and standardisation of products. Use of information and communication technology was to be promoted during the Plan period in this regard.
- The SGRY would be the single wage-employment programme. The programme would have three streams which would seek to address the need of rural infrastructure at the village level, ensure guaranteed employment of at least 100 days in areas facing chronic unemployment/migration and provide relief in natural calamities such as floods, droughts, earthquakes and other contingencies. The projects under SGRY would be chosen with a view to taking up schemes that enlarge the scope for increased economic activity.
- Access to land will be an important element in the poverty alleviation strategy. Tenancy reforms, record of rights of land owners and tenants, computerisation of land records, prevention of alienation of tribal lands, and issue of land

rights for women will be the major tenets of the land reform agenda.

- The promotion of a movement which enhances social capital and forges linkages with other formal and informal stakeholders engaged in developmental activities was to be a major thrust during the Plan. PRIs have created a space for the involvement of the community in governance. There is a need to provide greater attention to effective empowerment of PRIs. The Government recognises the necessity of building capabilities at the local levels for planning, implementation and monitoring of development programmes. These were to be undertaken on large scale during the Plan period.

ANNEXURE 6.1

Financial & Physical Performance under Poverty Alleviation Programmes IRDP/SGSY, JRY/JGSY and EAS during Eighth and Ninth Plan - Yearwise

(Rs. Crores)

Sl. No.	Years	IRDP/SGSY Total Allocation (Centre+ State)	Total Expenditure Swarozgaries	Lakh Families (Centre+ State)	JRY/JGSY Total Allocation	Total Expenditure	Employment (in Lakh Mandays)	EAS Total Allocation (Centre+ State)	Total Expenditure	Employment (in Lakh Mandays)
1	2	3	4	5	6	7	8	9	10	11
Eighth Plan										
1	1992-93	662.22	693.88	20.69	3169.05	2709.59	7821.02	0.00	-	
2	1993-94	1093.43	956.65	25.39	4059.42	3878.71	10258.4	0.00	183.75	494.74
3	1994-95	1098.22	1008.31	22.15	4376.92	4268.33	9517.07	0.00	1235.45	2729.56
4	1995-96	1097.21	1077.16	20.89	4848.70	4466.91	8958.25	0.00	1720.61	3465.27
5	1996-97	1097.21	1131.68	19.24	2236.79	2163.98	4006.32	0.00	2160.41	4030.02
Total		5048.29	4867.68	108.36	18690.88	17487.52	40561.06	0.00	5300.22	10719.6
Ninth Plan										
1	1997-98	1133.51	1109.54	17.07	2499.21	2439.38	3955.89	2460.48	2904.97	4717.74
2	1998-99	1456.28	1162.28	16.77	2597.03	2525.48	3766.41	2485.15	2882.18	4279.36
3	1999-2000	1472.34	959.86	9.34	2205.58	2032.45	2683.08	2431.46	2182.61	2786.17
4	2000-2001	1332.50	1116.27	10.30	2192.96	1929.23	2683.17	2082.27	1861.11	2183.92
5	2001-2002	774.50	555.15	6.25	2493.01	699.07	860.79	1730.92	530.92	666.27
Total		6169.13	4716.17	56.92	11687.93	9625.61	13949.34	11190.28	10361.79	14633.5

Note: • 2001-02 - SGSY - upto January, 2002 • 2001-02 - JGSY - upto October, 2001 • 2001-02 - EAS - upto September, 2001.
Source: Ministry of Rural Development.

Contributors

Aseem Shrivastava (aseem62@yahoo.com) is an independent writer.

C.P. Ravindranathan (ravindranathan@yahoo.com), a former Indian envoy to several countries, is a Professor at XIME, Bangalore.

Angus Deaton ("Alessandro Tarozzi" <taroz@econ.duke.edu>), Professor of Economics and International Affairs, Woodrow Wilson School and Department of Economics, Princeton University, 328 Wallace Hall, Princeton, NJ-08544.

Alessandro Tarozzi (taroz@econ.duke.edu), Assistant Professor of Economics, Duke University, P.O. Box 90097, Durham, NC-27708.

Tara Ramanathan (tramanat@ucsd.edu), B.A. (Economics), University of California at San Diego, La Jolla, CA 92093, National Institute of Urban Affairs, IHC, Lodhi Road, New Delhi-110003 (India).

Paramita Datta Dey, (pdey@niua.org), Senior Research Officer, National Institute of Urban Affairs, IHC, Lodhi Road, New Delhi-110003 (India).

V.K. Dhar (vdhar@niua.org), Professor (HUDCO Chair), National Institute of Urban Affairs, IHC, Lodhi Road, New Delhi-110003 (India).

Ruchira Sen (sen.ruchira@gmail.com), Summer Intern, May-July 2006, National Institute of Urban Affairs, IHC, Lodhi Road, New Delhi-110003 (India).

Nakul Kumar (nakul.kumar@gmail.com), Summer Intern, May-July 2006, National Institute of Urban Affairs, IHC, Lodhi Road, New Delhi-110003 (India).